BUILDING FOR GOD
GUIDELINES FROM THE BOOK OF NEHEMIAH

BUILDING FOR GOD

GUIDELINES FROM THE BOOK OF NEHEMIAH

JOHN WILLIAMS

Published by
GOSPEL FOLIO PRESS
304 Killaly St. W.
Port Colborne, ON L3K 6A6
CANADA

ISBN: 9781926765969

Cover design by Lisa Martin

All Scripture quotations from the
New International Version unless otherwise noted.

Printed in USA

DEDICATION

Dedicated to all those servants of the Lord who, like Nehemiah, are working faithfully and encouraging the people of God to build for Him.

CONTENTS

PREFACE

One of the purposes of the following chapters is to encourage spiritual wall-builders, gate hangers and any who, like Nehemiah and his fellow workers, are interested in doing a job for God. Although the Book of Nehemiah tells the story of events that happened millennia ago in Israel, it is strikingly contemporary. It has offered guidelines for individuals and churches in succeeding generations, including our own.

Despite his high political profile, Nehemiah's main concern was to encourage people to join hands with him in the service of God. His evident success stemmed not from his important contacts, nor from his "insider dealings," but from his moral and spiritual vision and integrity. Here was a man whose heart was in the right place; whose head was 'screwed on,' as we say, and whose hands were clean and available for God.

This story from Israel's past demonstrates that while spiritual renewal and revival ultimately come from the sovereign hand of God, they are enjoyed most by people who are available for God, and who have equipped themselves for service. Nehemiah warns us that when leaders compromise with evil, lose their vision, and fail to obey God's Word, spiritual malaise quickly sets in. On the other hand, when God's people neglect His truth and forsake His ways, their leaders become discouraged and apathetic.

In Nehemiah's day, the people were called to "live on the edge." They had none of the comfortable pew cushions of present day Christianity. Their enemies were close by, easily identified and threatening. In fact, they were just over the wall! Today, although our scenario may be different, the real enemy is the same. Evil is still well camouflaged in respectable, religious garb. We are all too easily seduced by the sensational, the commercial and the secular. As William Wordsworth put it, "The world is too much with us; late and soon, Getting and spending, we lay waste our powers."

Does it matter if we lower our standards, if we ease up on our commitment to the Lord and His truth, if we live "like the rest"? Well, Nehemiah tells us in no uncertain terms, it surely does matter! In point of fact, he tells us, —better, he shows us, — that our commitment to the Lord's work may involve, "throwing out some of the hoarded baggage of our traditions" and even "pulling out a few hairs!" However, more of that later.

The Book of Nehemiah offers little comfort to people who, for one reason or another, are content with the status quo, who are even willing to defend it against all comers. When we read about the sorry state of Jerusalem, we feel like asking Nehemiah, "Whatever went wrong? Why, after two earlier returns from exile, is there still so much rubbish, so many burned gates? Had the returned exiles become so discouraged that they simply downed tools and quit?" Had they settled down "at ease in Zion" and accepted the mounds of rubbish as part of the landscape?

Does this sound familiar? Have you run into people in your fellowship who resist changes and tell you, "We've always done it this way and we're quite happy. Why rock the boat?" This is not to deny that some traditions and methods have value. However, there are others which are both blocking the effective application of biblical principles, and hindering the work of God's Spirit. That is a serious situation and needs exposing and resisting. It sounds like the kind of problem Paul had in mind when he warned the friends at Thessalonica, *"Don't put out the Spirit's fire!"* (1 Thess. 5:19).

Fortunately, once Nehemiah arrived in Jerusalem, he was able to get people fired up and ready for action. Thank God for all such leaders among us today!

Like a good sermon, the Book of Nehemiah calls for a response. Here, for example, is the Lord's challenge through the prophet Malachi, a contemporary of Nehemiah's, as well as his companion and encourager: *"Test me in this,"* says the Lord Almighty, *"and see if I will not throw open the floodgates of heaven and pour you out so much blessing that you will not have room enough for it"* (Mal. 3: 10). I can imagine Nehemiah agreeing and saying a hearty, Amen. After all, he would be the first to tell us that when we are prepared to do our part, we can always count on God to do His. As the Psalmist reminds us, God can change our *"wailing to dancing"* and *"our problems to praise"* (Ps. 30:11).

—John Williams
Victoria, B.C. 2013

PART I

GOD AT WORK THROUGH PROBLEMS

"This is the word of the Lord to Zerubbabel: 'Not by might nor by power, but by My Spirit,' says the Lord Almighty. 'What are you, O mighty mountain? Before Zerubbabel you will become level ground. Then he will bring out the capstone with shouts of 'God bless it! God bless it!... Who despises the day of small things?'"

Zechariah 4:6-10

CHAPTER ONE
ONE MAN AND HIS GOD

Introduction

"When I heard these things, I sat down and wept. For some days I mourned and fasted and prayed before the God of heaven" (Neh. 1:4).

Nehemiah, cup-bearer turned statesman, was a man of considerable fortitude and practical common sense who lived in the fifth century B.C. Faced with a tough situation, he rolled up his sleeves and got involved not only in rebuilding the walls of Jerusalem but also in renewing his nation's spiritual and social life. He was a man of deep faith and prayer.

Congregations large and small can benefit greatly from the example of Nehemiah and from applying the principles unfolded in his book. Who knows what might happen if we took this bit of Biblical history seriously and made it a blueprint for our churches today?

This particular Bible book is not just a prosy narrative concerning some of the post-exilic happenings in Jerusalem. It is the story of "one man and his God." Furthermore, it offers a lively demonstration of what can happen when a group of dispirited nobodies, who are surrounded by enemies and heaps of rubbish, decide to dig in with their bare hands and to build for God's sake. As I read and reread this "primer on spiritual renewal," I looked for timeless guidelines that we might apply and benefit from today. Having been moved by what I read, I decided that an analytical approach might be the most useful. With this in mind, I drew four columns on a sheet of paper and headed them:

1. Problem
2. Reaction
3. Result
4. Lessons for Today

The more data I included under those four headings, the more it struck me that here are some answers for situations facing our local churches today! Now, without question, Nehemiah will cut us down to size and drive us to our knees. But, whoever imagined that the road to spiritual renewal and blessing would be smooth or easy?

As we examine Nehemiah's own words and methods, we will emphasize the practical rather than the theological message of his book. Later, we will pay some attention to what are usually described as "introduction and critical matters." At this point, we should note that much of the Book of Nehemiah consists of personal memoirs written in the first person. The middle section, chapters 8-12, is written in the third person, presumably by someone other than Nehemiah himself. These five chapters include a description of a national day of Scripture reading, a protracted prayer, a sworn national covenant and various records of names and family connections of the returned exiles.

We will take time to sift through the various problems Nehemiah faced and see how he dealt with them. This will help us uncover useful principles of recovery and apply them to our twenty first century church situation.

In the following series of short chapters we will break down the material under the four headings mentioned above. At the same time we will seek to walk in Nehemiah's moccasins, as the saying goes, and that, hopefully, will give us the feel of things and will help us avoid the mistake of measuring everything by the yardstick of contemporary method and custom.

At the outset we find out that Nehemiah was a well-to-do, respected member of the Jewish community, exiled in Babylon at the time of the ascendancy of the Persian Empire, circa the fifth century B.C. At the exact time our story commences he was in Susa, the summer residence of the reigning Persian monarch, King Artaxerxes I.

We also discover that Nehemiah's brother, Hanani, a leader of the Jewish community in Jerusalem, had just returned to Susa with a delegation of fellow Jews. The news he brought was most disconcerting. In fact, the more he talked the worse things sounded. Clearly the plight of Jerusalem and its environs had become lamentable. Presumably this was the result of enemy activity and because people had become discouraged and neglected the work.

The earlier, somewhat abortive, attempts to rebuild Jerusalem and re-establish worship there had, unfortunately, been frustrated. It seemed to have reached an impasse. Faced with such bad news, Nehemiah had several options. He could have done nothing, or, like a lot of us, simply played, 'Let's pretend everything in the garden is lovely!' Of course, he could have shrugged his shoulders and said, "I think Hanani is exaggerating, and in any case, it's not my problem. After all, I'm quite comfortable in my summer apartment here in Susa. Why get so excited? Let somebody else fix it." A further option might have been, for the sake of appearances, for Nehemiah to do something, even if it were totally irrelevant. That would at least salve his conscience while serving political ends! For example, why not organize a local chapter of "CRUMBS"—an acronym for, "The Committee for Recycling Used Materials and Bricks" for Jerusalem. Although that may sound completely ridiculous, it's surprising what some people get themselves involved in these days! "Doing something" evidently makes them feel good!

Fortunately, although Nehemiah could have avoided the issues that challenged him, he decided on a more positive approach. He chose nothing less than heart and hand involvement. He figured that his initial step must be to take careful inventory and get a first hand look at things. That's always a good place to start. Now, let's get into the story and see what happened and what we can learn. As we do so, let us pray Saul of Tarsus' famous prayer, *"Lord, what do you want me to do?"* (Acts 22:10).

CHAPTER TWO
"FIRST, THE BAD NEWS!"

"Those who survived the exile and are back in the province are in great trouble and disgrace. The wall of Jerusalem is broken down, and its gates have been burned with fire" Nehemiah 1:3

1. Problem

Anyone who had seen Jerusalem in all its glory, before the Babylonian captivity, would appreciate how depressing Hanani's first-hand report must have sounded to Nehemiah. "When I heard these things, I sat down and wept," Nehemiah recalls—perfectly understandable!

Just how dire the situation was, Nehemiah would find out later for himself. Here is his own eye-witness account,

> *"By night I went through the Valley Gate toward the Jackal Well and the Dung Gate, examining the walls of Jerusalem which had been broken down, and its gates, which had been destroyed by fire. Then I moved on toward the Fountain Gate and the King's Pool, but there was not enough room for my mount to get through; so I went up the Valley by night, examining the wall. Finally, I turned back and re-entered through the Valley Gate"* (Neh. 2:13-15).

In order to understand the seriousness of the situation facing Nehemiah, we need to remember that the walls and gates of an ancient city were absolutely essential for its security and survival. The walls kept out enemies and wild animals, and the gates were the seat of local government as well as the court for the administration of justice.

Faced with this sad situation, what would Nehemiah do? Time was of the essence.

2. Reaction

Nehemiah's first reaction was to weep, but fortunately that was not all he did! We read, *"For some days I mourned and fasted and prayed before the God of heaven"* (1:4). Clearly, this was no sudden emotional impulse on Nehemiah's part but a settled, ongoing experience which lasted at least eleven days. He was not only deeply moved but also intent on finding out the will of God and being ready for His service. Here was genuine humility and repentance. Nehemiah did not blame other people nor did he look for some convenient scapegoat. Instead he took the blame squarely on his own shoulders. He realized that the path to blessing involves not only prayer but also self denial, responsibility and hard work.

Incidentally, the prayers of Nehemiah are a study in themselves. There are at least ten of them recorded in the book that bears his name, illustrating various aspects of prayer. Prayer was as natural for Nehemiah as breathing. We will examine his prayer life in a separate chapter.

3. Result

It was in the month Kislev (November/December) 446 B.C. that Nehemiah received the sad news of Jerusalem's condition from his brother Hanani. Now, just four months later, in the month Nisan 445 B.C., he is finally, and somewhat surprisingly, given his opportunity to approach the Persian King, Artaxerxes I ("Longimanus" 464-423 B.C.). As already noted, Nehemiah was a member of the corp of individuals known as the royal cupbearers. These men were carefully screened for such trusted duty. This may account in part for the rather lengthy delay between the time Nehemiah received the news from Jerusalem and his opportunity to act upon it.

This story clearly intended to teach us that prayer changes things. Once he was in the King's presence, Nehemiah was not reluctant to express his concerns and to solicit Artaxerxes' help—but more of that later!

4. Lesson for Today

If we are honest, we have to admit that the problem facing too many of our churches today is, figuratively speaking, 'broken down walls and burned gates.' Here are some apparent evidences:

A diminishing of evangelistic zeal.

A tendency to rely on tradition rather than on God's truth;

An accommodation of moral standards;

An acceptance of entertaining programs rather than spiritual worship;

A willingness to accept "peace at any price" policies;

A selfish materialism which dilutes our sense of mission;

A lack of gifted, spiritual, servant leadership.

Of course, we are glad to say that this is not the whole picture. There are many fine churches that are winning souls and honouring the Lord and His Word. And of course, we thank God that there are always the prayer warriors who are making the difference.

Walls do two things: they exclude and they include. They keep out undesirable elements and they give security to those who are inside them. Clearly this is our need today. We must identify and exclude all that is of the world, the flesh, and the Devil. On the other hand, we must include all who love Christ and see to it that they feel wanted, loved, and cared for.

As we have discovered, the ancient city gate was the place where people could meet their elders and leaders, and receive wise advice and guidance for the everyday affairs of their lives. Surely this is a lesson for our local churches today. We do not need more executives to run the business of mega churches. We need men whose hearts are sensitive to people's needs, whose minds are aware of the truths of Scripture and who are like the men of Issachar *"who understood the times and knew what Israel should do"* (1 Chron. 12:32).

CHAPTER THREE
POISON IN THE CUP?

"In the month of Nisan in the twentieth year of King Artaxerxes, when wine was brought for him, I took the wine and gave it to the King. I had not been sad in his presence before; so the king asked me, 'Why does your face look so sad when you are not ill? This can be nothing but sadness of heart'".
Nehemiah 2:1-2

1. Problem

Nehemiah's second problem, although personal, was quite serious. As cupbearer of King Artaxerxes he held a particularly responsible position. It may not sound very important to us, but when we remember that the royal cupbearer was the man who actually handed the king's wine to him, we can understand that such a person must be beyond suspicion. In fact, Artaxerxes' father had been assassinated by poisoning. The poisoned cup was a favourite device for disposing of disliked despots!

So it was that on a certain day in Passover month, at the beginning of Artaxerxes' twentieth year, Nehemiah handed the king his wine. The king, ever alert for any suspicious circumstance, noticed that his cupbearer was looking sad. Immediately, Artaxerxes was on guard. *"Why does your face look so sad?"* he demanded. *"This can be nothing but sadness of heart."*

The king's question implied: What's wrong? Has somebody tried to bribe you to poison me? Such a question obviously had serious overtones and would immediately set Nehemiah back on his heels. What could he do to save the day, or was this his God-given moment of opportunity? He realized his secret was out. His 'poker face' betrayed his heart sickness. Would the king accept his story, or would Nehemiah, like many another unfortunate cupbearer before him, be summarily dismissed or even sent to the gallows? Persian despots were notorious for their capricious actions! Do you remember that saying about *"the law of the Medes and Persians that does not change"?* (cf. Dan. 6:12).

2. Reaction

Although fully aware of the serious danger he was in, Nehemiah refused to push the panic button. Instead, he did what came naturally for him. Resting his faith in God, he prayed. His next step was to tell Artaxerxes that his sad face reflected no menacing motives. He was downcast because of tragic news he had received about his ancestral city and home.

"Well, what do you expect me to do about it?" shouted the king, rather agitatedly. At this crucial moment Nehemiah made his famous response. We read, *"...Then I prayed to the God of heaven, and I answered the king..."* (Neh. 2:4-5)

Faced with an extremely hazardous situation and with no text-book precedent, God's servant knew exactly what to do. Quick as a wink, Nehemiah shot up a prayer to Heaven, then calmly and deliberately made his request of King Artaxerxes.

3. Result

Just as his earlier prayer (1:1-11) had opened the door into King Artaxerxes' presence giving Nehemiah his opportunity to intercede on behalf of his people, so now his "telegram prayer" was answered with even more dramatic results. Typically, Nehemiah is quick to acknowledge this. We hear him explain. *"And because the gracious hand of my God was upon me, the king granted my request"* (Neh. 2:8). It is doubtful whether even Nehemiah could have guessed just how far-reaching and significant God's answer would turn out to be. To help us appreciate this, we recall Gabriel's words to Daniel:

> *"Seventy 'sevens' are decreed for your people and your holy city to finish transgression, to put an end to sin, to atone for wickedness, to bring in everlasting righteousness, to seal up vision and prophecy and to anoint the most holy.*

> *"Know and understand this: From the issuing of the decree*
> *to restore and rebuild Jerusalem until the Anointed One,*
> *the ruler, comes, there will be seven 'sevens' and sixty two*
> *'sevens.' It will be rebuilt with streets and a trench but in*
> *times of trouble"* (Dan. 9:24-25).

The key phrase here, for our present study, reads, *"From the issuing of the decree to restore and rebuild Jerusalem."* Now it is generally agreed that there were several of these so-called 'decrees to build.' For example, there was the decree of Cyrus the Great (559-530 B.C.) mentioned in 2 Chronicles 36:22 and Ezra 1:1-4. This occasioned Sheshbazzar's expedition which is referred to in Ezra 2. (It is accepted that this was the same person who is also called Zerubbabel).

Then there was the decree of Darius the Great (521-486 B.C.) issued at the beginning of his reign, which appears to have been a confirmation of Cyrus' earlier decree. Third, there was the decree of Artaxerxes given to Ezra 458 B.C. (Ezra 7:12). Finally, there was Artaxerxes I's second decree issued to Nehemiah in 445 B.C, the one mentioned in Nehemiah 2:1-8. Evangelical scholars are generally agreed this latter decree is the one referred to in Daniel 9:25. This gives us the *terminus a quo* (the starting point) for Daniel's seventy 'heptads' or 'weeks of years.'

Incidentally, it has been pointed out that if we take the earlier decree of 458 B.C, as our *terminus a quo* and use the solar calendar, we arrive at the same *terminus ad quem* (final date) as we would by making the 445 B.C. our starting point but following the lunar calendar. This may not seem important, but if we interpret the years of Daniel's prophecy literally, then the *terminus ad quem* becomes A.D. 30—the time of our Lord's crucifixion. For a detailed discussion of this interpretation see Sir Robert Anderson's book, *The Coming Prince.*

In light of the foregoing details, the answer to Nehemiah's prayer is all the more remarkable. Of course, some scholars regard the preceding chronology as far-fetched but it seems that the burden of proof remains with them. After all, there is an obvious literalness about Daniel's understanding of Jeremiah's seventy year captivity prophecy, so why not a literal chronology here? Furthermore, in Revelation 11:2, the equivalent of Daniel's "half week" is given as forty-two months or 1260 days—(cf. 12:6;13:5 etc. Dan. 9:2; Jer. 29:10 and Matt. 24:15).

4. Lessons for Today

The lesson here is so obvious it hardly needs comment. What do we do when faced with sudden and serious problems? These may relate to our personal life, our family, our church, our job or our health! Do we fall apart; retire into our shell; take it out on other people, or just try to tough it out? Nehemiah shows us the way. His advice for us would be, Take it to the Lord in prayer.

We are not told precisely what Nehemiah prayed for. His was certainly not a long-winded intercession. He probably said or simply thought, "Help, Lord!" or, "Please let me say the right thing!" Remember, Nehemiah did not even know about that wonderful promise Jesus gave his disciples, *"When you are brought before synagogues, rulers and authorities, do not worry about how you will defend yourselves or what you will say, for the Holy Spirit will teach you at that time what you should say"* (Luke 12:11-12).

Of course, Nehemiah certainly believed in the same God and acted on the same faith principle. This is surely a great encouragement to us. It is always wise to think and to pray before you speak. Nehemiah knew what was needed and prayed accordingly, even if he had no clue as to the outcome. He was content to leave that with the Lord. In his very helpful little book, *Prayer Secrets*, (Marshall, Morgan and Scott, London), Guy King calls Nehemiah's prayer "the sky telegram." He suggests that it met "A Sudden Need", it called for "Swift Action", and it involved a "Short Message". Sounds like three good headings for a sermon!

CHAPTER FOUR
STICKS AND STONES

"Also our enemies said, 'Before they know it or see us, we will be right there among them and will kill them and put an end to the work'"   Nehemiah 4:11

1. Problem

Nehemiah's next problem was to become his perennial problem. Month after month, year after year, he faced the determined assaults of three enemy leaders who were bent on thwarting his every effort. Identified quite early in the story, their names recur with monotonous regularity: Sanballat the Horonite, governor of Samaria; Tobiah the Ammonite, usually known as governor of Trans-Jordan; and Geshem the Arab who seems to have wielded power in the area we know as Saudi Arabia.

Reading between the lines, it seems that the opposition of this enemy group was both politically and economically motivated. They saw Nehemiah's success as a threat to their power and purse. As a result, they determined to launch various kinds of attacks in order to destroy him and his associates. It is informative to join together the various accounts of their attacks in order to form a clear picture of what was going on.

The first encounter occurred almost immediately upon Nehemiah's arrival in Jerusalem. We read,

> *"But when Sanballat the Horonite, Tobiah the Ammonite official and Geshem the Arab heard about it, they mocked and ridiculed us. 'What is this you are doing?' they asked. 'Are you rebelling against the King?'"* (Neh. 2:19).

The next hint of trouble comes at the half-way stage of the building of the walls of Jerusalem. We read,

"When Sanballat heard that we were rebuilding the wall, he became angry and was greatly incensed. He ridiculed the Jews and in the presence of his associates and the army of Samaria, he said, 'What are those feeble Jews doing? Will they restore their wall? Will they offer sacrifices? Will they finish in a day? Can they bring stones back to life from those heaps of rubble—burned as they are?'

"Tobiah the Ammonite, who was at his side, said, 'What they are building—if even a fox climbed up on it, he would break down their wall of stones!'" (Neh. 4:1-3).

Things became even uglier once all the gaps in the wall were filled in. At this point we read,

"But when Sanballat, Tobiah, the Arabs, the Ammonites and the men of Ashdod heard that the repairs to Jerusalem's walls had gone ahead and that the gaps were being closed, they were very angry. They all plotted together to come and fight against Jerusalem and stir up trouble against it" (Neh. 4:7-8).

Surprisingly, at this point in the story, the "cold war" tactics of Sanballat, Tobiah and Geshem abruptly halted. Recognizing that their frontal assault and propaganda were not working but rather galvanizing Jewish resistance, they initiated a policy of detente. Their new stratagem was "seduction by social infiltration"—a policy similar to that of Balak and Balaam, of an earlier generation (cf. Num. 22-23).

Although this ruse was effective at first, Nehemiah soon recognized it for what it was and, by God's grace, countered it. We'll consider more of that in our next chapter. At this point let's see how God's people responded to the enemies' assaults.

2. Reaction

Faced with enemy opposition and ridicule, Nehemiah reacted in a variety of ways. First, he expressed his absolute confidence in God. Second, he assured his enemies that since the Jews were

God's servants doing God's work, nothing would prevent their success. Third, he refused to be intimidated; he stood up for his people's rights and rebutted the enemy claims (cf. 2:20). Fourth, he committed the matter to God in prayer. It is as though he was saying, "This is not our problem, God, it's yours!"

Speaking of Nehemiah's prayer life, we notice here one of the recurring features of his prayers, namely, his imprecatory prayers. Prayer for God's judgment on one's enemies is found frequently in David's Psalms. This may seem strange to us, especially in light of Jesus' words about praying for our enemies (cf. Luke 7:27-28; 11:4). We will look at them again in a later chapter.

Nehemiah's other reaction to enemy threats was quite simply expressed in his own words, *"But we prayed to our God and posted a guard day and night to meet this threat"* (Neh. 4:9). Nehemiah was practical, if nothing else. He did not believe in asking God to do for him and his people what they were perfectly capable of doing themselves. Furthermore, he saw the folly of prayer divorced from common sense—a fact many Christians seem loathe to learn!

3. Result

Nothing is more likely to unite and galvanize people to action than the appearance and threat of a common enemy. This is precisely what happened in Jerusalem as Nehemiah commenced his wall-building project. Faced with the taunts and threats of Sanballat, Tobiah and Geshem, the returned exiles were drawn together in the common cause and spurred into action. Social, ecclesiastical, educational, cultural and whatever other prejudices and petty things dividing them were set aside. As one man, they enthusiastically gave themselves to the work at hand.

Nehemiah chapter three makes interesting reading. We discover that Eliashib, the high priest and his fellow priests, pitched in with everyone else to build the Sheep Gate and the adjacent section of the wall. Next to them were the men of Jericho, then Zaccur, the son of Imri, and so on. The Jeshanah Gate was repaired by one group, the Valley Gate by another, the Dung Gate by another, the Water Gate by another, the Horse

Gate by another, the Inspection Gate by another, the Sheep Gate by another—and so it went! (See diagram in Appendix Three).

As the narrative of the wall-building unfolds, it is fascinating to notice some of the incidental, yet revealing, details. We discover for example, that goldsmiths, perfume makers and merchants, men who were unused to soiling their hands with heavy manual labour, all pulled their weight. One man called Shallum who was "ruler of a half-district of Jerusalem" not only engaged in building work himself but brought his daughters along to help him. There was only one dissonant note. It reads,

"The next section was repaired by the men of Tekoa, but their nobles would not put their shoulders to the work under their supervisors" (Neh. 3:5). There are always a few who seem to march to the beat of a different drummer, who consider themselves a cut above the rest and refuse to cooperate. However, in this particular project, they turned out to be a minority, the exception that proved the rule.

One further result is worth noting. The enemy was frustrated. All he could do was threaten and bluster. Amazed at the progress of the wall building and the determination of the builders he was reduced to name-calling and innuendo.

4. Lessons for Today

Clearly, there are lessons to be learned from this part of the story. For example, when the people of God are faced with seemingly insurmountable obstacles and threatened by their enemies, the key to victory lies in a prayerful commitment to unity in the work of God. The secret of success is involvement. Once people see a need and realize that they must stand shoulder to shoulder to meet it, things begin to happen. Each of us needs a challenge and an opportunity. It is amazing what can be accomplished when every member, imbued with a servant spirit, is willing to use his or her gift for the forwarding of the work of God. Today, when the Christian Church is being assailed by determined and diabolically inspired forces, she still has recourse to that most potent tool—"the weapon of all-prayer," to use John Bunyan's phrase. There can be no question, the forces of evil are both subtle and strong, and their attacks on Christians are concerted and continuous. Satan has powerful lobbyists among the media moguls! However, we need not run away nor wilt before the lies and insinuations that are hurled at us. While we must not descend to the name-calling, pressure tactics of our enemies, by the same token, we must be willing to take a firm stand for truth and righteousness. Let us not be cowed by the vociferous vituperations of a godless, immoral minority. We can and should, by all the legal and reasonable means at our disposal, stand up for truth and go on the offensive for what is right—without being offensive!

We are not obliged to condone promiscuity and pornography in the name of tolerance when we know that such life-styles are not only an affront to God and His Word but destructive of family life and human society. Christians must both speak out and use their civil freedoms to act against these Satanic perversions. What about abortions? Can we Christians pussy-foot around while millions of defenceless little people are dismembered and thrown in the garbage to be incinerated? Such heartless cruelty is not only a blot on the human race, it is a fist in the face of God! Were Nehemiah around today, there is no doubt he would not only pray for our confused society but he would also take steps to mobilize the people of God against the blatant, pernicious evils all around us. He would be unimpressed with the specious arguments and excuses put forward in the name of 'human rights and personal liberty.' There is no liberty without true justice and morality.

CHAPTER FIVE
FIFTH COLUMN TACTICS

"Sanballat and Geshem sent me this message: 'Come, let us meet together in one of the villages on the plain of Ono.' But they were scheming to harm me; so I sent messengers to them with this reply: 'I am carrying on a great project and cannot go down. Why should the work stop while I leave it and go down to you?'"   Nehemiah 6:2-3

1. Problem

Having survived the open aggression of the enemy, Nehemiah and the people of God were now being harassed by enemy schemes of infiltration and seduction. It has long been recognized that propaganda and the spreading of disinformation are effective weapons of warfare. Modern adversaries spend millions on ploys such as harassment.

Nehemiah's enemies aimed to make right appear to be wrong, truth appear to be falsehood, and evil appear to be good! Their scheme was to talk peace while stock-piling weapons, to offer detente while planning aggression. All of this certainly sounds familiar to our ears today.

Fortunately, Nehemiah immediately recognized this devious tactic and exposed it. He recognized that having failed in their frontal assault, Sanballat and Tobiah were now conducting a two-pronged offensive. On the one hand they were attempting to infiltrate and defeat the Jewish community at large. On the other, they were conspiring to destroy Nehemiah himself. Their idea was to flatter him, then inveigle him into attending a "summit meeting." On at least four separate occasions they invited him to confer with them *"in one of the villages on the plain of Ono"* (6:2), a place certainly well named! Fortunately, Nehemiah did not take their bait. He recognized—as he puts it,—that *"they were scheming to harm me"*. His answer was:—"O, No!"

Incensed by Nehemiah's refusal, Sanballat became furious and was forced to tip his hand. Thereupon, he despatched an aide with an "unsealed letter" in which he charged Nehemiah with outrageous schemes of sedition and political revolt. This clever stratagem also failed lamentably. Here is the content of this letter,

> *"It is reported among the nations—and Geshem says it is true—that you and the Jews are plotting to revolt, and therefore you are building the wall. Moreover, according to these reports you are about to become their king, and have even appointed prophets to make the proclamation about you in Jerusalem: 'There is a king in Judah! Now this report will get back to the king; so come, let us confer together'"* (Neh. 6:6, 7).

Having failed to shake Nehemiah's resolve, the enemy pulled another tactic from his "bag of dirty tricks." Sanballat and Tobiah hired a man called Shemaiah—probably a Jewish priest. Feigning to be under some kind of household arrest, this character warned Nehemiah that his own, as well as Nehemiah's, life was in danger. He therefore suggested that Nehemiah rendezvous with him in the Temple—a recognized place of sanctuary. Nehemiah saw that this too was a plot—a further attempt to intimidate and embarrass him. He declined to cooperate and in so doing probably saved his life. We will look at the details of his response later.

Another enemy stratagem involved people who were quite highly placed in Nehemiah's forces. This of course was very serious and unfortunately quite successful. Tobiah managed to pull off an incredible 'double coup.' First, he set out to win the hand of the daughter of Shecaniah, a leading Jewish citizen whose son Shemaiah worked in Nehemiah's 'department of defence' (cf. Neh. 6:18 and 3:29). Second, he married off his son Jehohanan to the daughter of Meshullam, another leading Jew who had actually helped Nehemiah build the Jerusalem wall (cf. Neh. 3:4, 30).

Obviously Nehemiah had to tread carefully. Not only was there the danger of his plans being leaked to the enemy but there was also the chance of enemy disinformation being fed to the upper echelons of his forces to undermine their morale. A lesser man might have been daunted by such infamy, but not Nehemiah.

2. Reaction

It becomes obvious at this point in the story that the cunning and duplicity of Sanballat and Tobiah were matched only by the divinely-bestowed insight of Nehemiah, not to mention his personal integrity. When invited to the so-called "Ono summit" Nehemiah declined with thanks. Once again, he displayed considerable courage and discernment. Try to imagine the situation. It must have been an attractive offer for Nehemiah to take off the sweaty overalls in which he had been obliged to work, eat and sleep for so long. Why not take time off and enjoy a comfortable furlough with the political leaders of the surrounding nations?

However, Nehemiah showed once again that he lived by different standards and subscribed to a different set of values. I like his reply, *"I am carrying on a great project and cannot go down. Why should the work stop while I leave it and go down to you?"* (Neh. 6:3). He showed this same perceptiveness in his reply to Shemaiah the son of Delaiah, who wanted to meet with him in the Temple. What could be better than a conversation in the temple precincts, especially since it was a place of sanctuary?

Fortunately, Nehemiah 'smelled a rat,' as we say. Aware of the Law and of priestly protocol which permitted only priests to access that particular Temple area, he declined this further invitation. He may have remembered what happened to the unfortunate King Uzziah several centuries before (cf. 2 Chron. 26:16ff). In any case, he escaped these attempts to entrap and discredit him (cf. Neh. 6:13).

It is also interesting to see Nehemiah stand up to his enemies' attempt at defaming him. Not only did he not fall for their trickery but he calls them the liars that they are. Their story was a sheer fabrication and Nehemiah was not afraid to tell them so. At the same time he fired off one of his brief prayers: *"Now strengthen my hands"* (6:9). It was as if he was saying: Well Lord I have spent the last bullet in my clip. Now it's over to you!

3. Result

The result is described as follows:

> *"So the wall was completed on the twenty-fifth of Elul, in fifty-two days. When all our enemies heard about this, all the surrounding nations were afraid and lost their self-confidence, because they realized that this work had been done with the help of our God"* (Neh. 6:15-16).

Here is a clear illustration of the principle expressed in the Book of Proverbs, *"When a man's ways are pleasing to the Lord, he makes even his enemies to be at peace"* (Prov. 16:7).

Precautions were taken; guards and gatekeepers were put in place to keep out any intruders. There is an interesting note in Nehemiah 7:3. It tells us that guards were posted—"some at their posts and some near their own houses." Nehemiah recognized that it was good psychological strategy to have men guard their own homes and neighbourhoods. Furthermore, he then took inventory to make sure that there were sufficient people living in Jerusalem as well as in the more distant suburbs. This of course was a matter of security and shared responsibility.

After the people were safely settled and the defences in place, Nehemiah then saw to it that worship was reinstated. This emphasis is important for all who seek to forward the work of God. Priority was given to the Word of God and its careful exposition. Ezra the scribe read from the Scriptures hours on end. The people not only listened but responded with enthusiasm. One practical result was the restoration of the Feast of Tabernacles. The population worshiped together with holy joy. They shared a time of confession, then praised the Lord and rededicated themselves to His service.

4. Lessons for Today

How Nehemiah reacted to the subtle criticism of his foes and their attempt to infiltrate his ranks can help us today. So often our problems are like his. It is not the attacks from outside the Church that are so hard to take after all; they are to be expected. It is what the old hymn calls "fightings within" that are harder to deal with. It is tough when we discover that friends we thought we could count on prove disloyal. For example, what happens when the church treasurer embezzles the offering; when the youth leader divorces his wife for another woman; or when a respected deacon begins disseminating false teaching? These situations are always a challenge. We may decide to sweep things under the rug but this will not help. Such difficulties must be courageously faced and dealt with. Sometimes it may even be necessary to do some rebuking *"before all, so that the rest may fear"* —to cite Paul's words (see 1 Tim. 5:20).

It will certainly be a salutary thing to keep an open heart before the Lord. This will help us sense trouble when something is awry. As Nehemiah discovered, it is always a wise safeguard to familiarize ourselves with the Word of God. Then, when something is brought forward which is contrary to its precepts, we shall be able to recognize it for what it is and not be all too easily taken in. It is the doctor who knows his anatomy charts that is good at diagnosis! Satan has his Sanballat's around today. He is a master of subterfuge.

We can be easily snared by attractive offers to raise our personal or our church's profile. There are all kinds of appealing suggestions to compromise and join hands with unbelievers for political ends. Church leaders and members will be well advised to stay with God-given principles and to keep clear of compromise. We need to beware of glossy-ad promises of "instant success" or "instant spirituality." As an old preacher advised, "Make sure it's the Shepherd's voice, not that of a hireling."

Another lesson we need to keep in mind is this: difficulties and problems are not necessarily bad for us, nor should we vainly suppose that God is obliged to get us out of every predicament we find ourselves in. Faced with the subtle and subversive attacks of his enemies, Nehemiah did not run away, nor did he blame God for the problems besetting him. He faced up to things squarely and, having prayed and encouraged himself in the Lord, he got going. That is the challenge he offers us.

CHAPTER SIX
"RUBBISH, RUBBISH EVERYWHERE."

"Meanwhile the people in Judah said, 'The strength of the labourers is giving out, and there is so much rubble that we cannot rebuild the wall.'"   Nehemiah 4:10

1. Problem

The first blush of enthusiasm was fading. The enemy propaganda machine was working overtime, churning out rumours and threats. The wall was only half built and there were still mounds of rubbish everywhere. This was the scenario as Nehemiah's rebuilding project ground forward, threatening to come to a halt. Understandably, people were becoming discouraged. Not only were they physically exhausted but, once they had finished their work shift on the wall, they were expected to stand guard duty also. They had already put in weeks of backbreaking labour and, as far as could be seen, had made only a dent in what needed to be done.

Initially everyone had been enthused. In the early days people seemed to have boundless energy and undiminished faith. Now things had changed. Some, no doubt, wondered whether the project was really worthwhile. Why not accept the enemy's offers of help? Why be so resolute in rejecting any degree of compromise?

What was Nehemiah to do? Certainly the people were discouraged and as surely as their enthusiasm waned, just as surely the enemy's efforts appeared to be more determined. The situation was deteriorating and obviously the problems would not go away on their own. Some decisive action was called for.

2. Reaction

The true measure of a leader is not how he functions when everything is rosy and the work is advancing. The real test of his mettle is how he copes when people's spirits are down and the mounds of rubbish are increasing. It was precisely at this point that Nehemiah came through.

The first thing he did was to make a careful assessment of the situation. Then he called everyone together, leaders and people alike, and gave them a pep talk in which he suggested seven things. Here are Nehemiah's pointers—if we may paraphrase him.

Number 1

"Let's get our priorities straight. Recognize that however strong our enemy appears to be and however massive the project—God is greater and His resources unlimited"(4:14). That sounds like some words from Tate and Brady's famous hymn, "Through all the changing scenes of life"—

> "Fear him ye saints: and you will then
>   Have nothing else to fear;
>   Make you His service your delight,
>   Your wants shall be his care."

Number 2

"Realize that we are all in this together: each one of us depends on the other. This is not just a civic project. What we are doing is for the security of our families and our future as a nation" (v. 14).

Number 3

"We must review our defences and carefully delegate responsibilities. The most vulnerable places will require more man power" (v. 13).

Number 4

"While our confidence is in the Lord, we must be alert and do our part, recognizing that we are engaged in warfare as well as wall-building. Every able-bodied man must carry his trowel and wear his sword" (v. 17). Oliver Cromwell put it this way, "Trust in God and keep your powder dry!"

Number 5

"We must develop effective communication lines and be on our toes in case of any emergency" (v. 19-20).

Number 6

"We must stick together all the time, not just in the brighter moments but in the dark ones as well" (v. 21-22).

Number 7

"Each of us must face up to his or her responsibility and say to ourselves. It all depends on me—and I depend on God" (v. 15).

3. Result

The result of Nehemiah's strategy is summed up for us in verse 15, *"When our enemies heard that we were aware of their plot and that God had frustrated it, we all returned to the wall, each to his own work."*

Again we see that there is nothing like a challenge to motivate people. However, it is worth noticing that, in the flush of their early success and the frustration of the adversary, the people of God could not let up and become careless. It was made clear that, once begun, the work must be carried through. Nehemiah's plans were not only well conceived but carefully executed, and so produced results. We can certainly learn from his example. We see that there was a wise delegating of responsibility. Half of the men were armed and equipped, then stationed on guard duty, while the other half carried on with the actual building of the wall. Of course, the builders were armed as well, just in case! All duties were shared and the leaders, including Nehemiah himself, were required to make a 24/7 commitment to the work in hand. It seems that despite their added responsibilities and lack of leisure time, the people managed to keep going. In fact, they completed the work in record time.

The results Nehemiah achieved remind us that people need to be "stretched" physically and spiritually. Christians work best when they are properly directed, given tangible goals and challenged to achieve.

4. Lessons for Today

Today, unfortunately, many Christians, including some who are called to offer leadership, equate success with big numbers, smiling faces and glamorous projects. However, real life, whether at the personal, domestic or local church level, is not like that. More often than not, in the nitty-gritty of experience—"the trivial round and common task," to use the hymn writer's phrase—life tends to be unfinished walls, mounds of rubbish, gossip, rumour, innuendo and discouragement. Indeed, in the metaphor of our story, we are faced with Christians who are not only surrounded by rubbish but prefer it that way. Some even object to having the rubble of their comfortable customs and traditions disturbed. What are we to do under such circumstances? We shall not go far wrong if we follow Nehemiah's example. As a personally involved, committed leader, he renewed people's confidence in God and challenged them with their responsibility to work.

Many established churches are faced with the unhappy situation in which a minority of the members are struggling to do everything while the majority sit back and simply suggest how it should be done! As someone observed, some local churches are like a Saturday afternoon football game where the team members out on the field are getting worn out trying to move the ball forward, while the noisy spectators in the bleachers yell out their advice but do nothing to help! The sooner we recognize that the Christian life is neither a picnic nor a game but warfare, the sooner the work of God will be done. Certainly discouragement is a tough syndrome to break, but most people respond to a fresh challenge. Such a challenge must remind us not only of God's resources, but of the seriousness of dodging our God-given responsibilities. It must also be accompanied by a workable plan. That's where Nehemiah scored success. And so shall we by the grace of God!

CHAPTER SEVEN
FIGHTING
THE WRONG ENEMY

"Now the men and their wives raised a great outcry against their Jewish brothers. Some were saying, 'We and our sons and daughters are numerous; in order for us to eat and stay alive, we must get grain.' Others were saying, 'We are mortgaging our fields, our vineyards and our homes to get grain during the famine.'

"Still others were saying, 'We have had to borrow money to pay the king's tax on our fields and vineyards. Although we are the same flesh and blood as our countrymen and though our sons are as good as theirs, yet we have to subject our sons and daughters to slavery'".

Nehemiah 5:1-5

1. Problem

There are few things more spiritually enervating and physically draining than trying to encourage people to get a job done while they squabble among themselves. This was Nehemiah's next problem as he pressed forward with his wall-building project.

This particular problem developed out of economic necessity. It seems that some of the returned exiles had fallen on hard times. There had evidently been a famine and as a result many became poor and found it necessary to mortgage their lands to pay for food. Compounding the problem was the behaviour of other people who, despite the straightened circumstances of the times, remained reasonably well off. These fortunate few were taking advantage of their impoverished neighbours. Not only were they enslaving their fellow Jews and their children in lieu of payment of debts, they were also charging usurious interest on financial loans. Some of the poorest returnees were actually stealing food to keep themselves and their families alive.

Undoubtedly the problem took time to develop but the longer it went unchecked the more it festered. It threatened social harmony, destroyed family happiness, played into the hands of the enemy and, of course, bid fair to halting work on the walls. Something must be done and done soon!

2. Reaction

Nehemiah's immediate reaction was one of anger—not resentment but righteous indignation. Obviously he felt something had to be done. His first step was to summon a sort of town meeting in order to give the matter wide exposure and to call for maximum involvement. Having assembled the crowd, Nehemiah developed his attack along three lines. First, he pointed out the unreasonableness of enslaving fellow Jews. After all, one of the secondary projects of the wall-builders was to secure the release of Jews from their servitude to Gentiles!

Second, he declared that what they were doing was morally wrong and contrary to God's Law. He, no doubt, had in mind scriptures such as Exodus 22:25-27 and Leviticus 25:36 which prohibited charging interest to those who are poor or hungry.

Third, he cited his own example of freely making funds and goods available to the needy. Incidentally, just how personally and generously involved Nehemiah was is evident from the inventory given in chapter 5:17-18. Here is an excerpt from it:

> "Furthermore, an hundred and fifty Jews and officials ate at my table, as well as those who came to us from the surrounding nations. Each day one ox, six choice sheep and some poultry were prepared for me, and every ten days an abundant supply of wine of all kinds. In spite of all this, I never demanded the food allotted to the governor, because the demands were heavy on these people."

Next, he exposed what was wrong, demanded that it stop forthwith and insisted that full compensation be made. Furthermore, he required that land-owners and legislators alike take a solemn public oath to cease and desist from their wrong doing. He even threatened them with divine retribution and judgment

3. Result

The result of Nehemiah's action was as impressive as it was immediate. The simple words of Scripture say it all and need no commentary. *"At this the whole assembly said, 'Amen,' and praised the Lord. And the people did as they had promised"* (Neh. 5:13b).

4. Lesson for Today

Anyone who has faced disunity or dissent in a local church, will know that the worst thing that can happen is for the matter to be swept under the rug. Such problems do not vanish, they just continue to multiply. Sooner or later they resurface only to cause more serious hurt and division.

Elders and leaders in Christian churches will be well advised to do what Nehemiah did. First, and this is so important, taking a page out of Nehemiah's book, they will make sure that their own behaviour is above reproach, a pattern for the rest of the congregation. Second, they will bring matters out into the open and, at the risk of some temporary embarrassment and ill-feeling, they will expose whatever it is that is causing discord, then seek to address it. Third, they will make it clear to everyone that their action is in accordance with Scripture and is being carried out on the basis of transparent, ethical principles. If miscreants need to be rebuked, leaders must not flinch from doing it. Should such persons prove to be intractable, they should be disciplined. This will be for their own good with a view to their restoration to fellowship, and for the solidarity and blessing of the whole assembly (cf. Gal. 6:1).

Such a careful approach after prayer, will not only help to right what is wrong but may very well result in progress, as in Nehemiah's case. The judging of sin and resultant repentance will bring glory to God. Christian leadership has its price. It is no sinecure nor is it for people who are trying to win popularity contests!

CHAPTER EIGHT
MAKING ROOM
FOR GOD

"But while all this was going on, I was not in Jerusalem, for in the thirty-second year of Artaxerxes king of Babylon, I had returned to the king. Some time later I asked his permission and came back to Jerusalem. Here I learned about the evil thing Eliashib had done in providing Tobiah a room in the courts of the house of God. I was greatly displeased and threw all Tobiah's household goods out of the room. I gave orders to purify the rooms, and then I put back into them the equipment of the house of God, with the grain offerings and the incense".

Nehemiah 13:6-9

1. Problem

This particular situation had developed during Nehemiah's absence from Jerusalem. He had evidently gone on a visit to Babylon to give a firsthand report to King Artaxerxes. It's the old story that, "While the cat's away, the mice play." The problem involved Eliashib the High Priest. We are not given the details but it seems that Eliashib, who had been one of Nehemiah's loyal helpers while the wall was being built (3:1), had entered into some sort of alliance with Tobiah. Perhaps inflated by a sense of his own importance, as a kind of stand-in for the absent governor, or influenced by a bribe, Eliashib had done his people a great disservice. He had provided Tobiah with a large room in the Temple. This of course was not only unbelievably disloyal but blatantly illegal. It was tantamount to his becoming an accessory to an act of sacrilege.

Eliashib's folly was all the more dangerous for two reasons. First, Tobiah was not a member of the priesthood but was the arch-enemy of the returning exiles. It is hard to imagine what Eliashib was thinking or how he got away with his perfidy.

The situation was further aggravated by the fact that the room Eliashib had allocated Tobiah was part of the Temple treasury in which the tithes and offerings of Israel were usually stored. With this room occupied, there was nowhere to store the tithes and so people stopped bringing them.

Of course, the sequence of events may have been the other way round. Perhaps because of their spiritual malaise and apostasy, the people were not bringing their tithes and offerings and so the tithe room was standing empty. In which case perhaps Eliashib rented the space out to Tobiah in order to compensate for lack of income. In any event, Eliashib was not alone in his dereliction of duty.

A further key to our understanding of the situation can be found in the phrase, *"the portions assigned to the Levites had not been given to them and all the Levites and singers responsible for the service had gone back to their own fields"* (13:10). Here was yet another link in the chain of spiritual declension. Since the people had stopped giving and the treasury was empty, the Lord's servants were starving and had to abandon the service of God in order to eke out a living for themselves and their families. Clearly, the problem was serious and compounded. Once more, something had to be done.

2. Reaction

Upon his return to Jerusalem, Nehemiah quickly sized up the situation and took action. He placed the blame squarely on Eliashib and gave all the responsible leaders a good dressing down. Next, he ordered the cleansing and reconsecration of the Temple treasury, then summoned the Levites back to their posts. It would seem that Tobiah, anticipating Nehemiah's arrival, had discreetly made himself scarce but in his hurry to vacate the sacred premises had left his household effects behind. However, that was no problem for Nehemiah. He quickly took things in hand and personally tossed Tobiah's stuff out of the temple treasury, lock, stock and barrel! (Neh. 13:8). It must have been quite an exciting spectacle—'a moving day' in more ways than one!

Fortunately, Nehemiah was not alone in his house cleaning. He had an enthusiastic associate and ally in the person of Malachi the prophet. Now, although the Book of Nehemiah is quite widely separated from the prophecy of Malachi in the arrangement of the English Old Testament canon, these two men were contemporaries. Incidentally, the Book of Malachi comes before Ezra and Nehemiah in the Hebrew canon. Recognizing this, we shall better understand the significance of Malachi's friendship with Nehemiah, as well as his following, strident tones:

> *"'...return to me and I will return to you,' says the LORD Almighty.*
>
> *'But you ask, 'How are we to return?'*
>
> *Will a man rob God? Yet you rob me.*
>
> *But you ask, 'How do we rob you?'*
>
> *In tithes and offerings. You are under a curse—the whole nation of you—because you are robbing me. Bring the whole tithe into the storehouse, that there may be food in my house. Test me in this,' says the Lord Almighty, 'and see if I will not throw open the floodgates of heaven and pour out so much blessing that you will not have room enough for it'"* (Mal. 3:7b-10).

Now that Tobiah's furniture was out in the street, so to speak, there was room for the Lord's tithe. To put the prophet's message in contemporary jargon, Malachi says, "Put your money where your mouth is; then stand back and watch out for God's blessing!"

3. Result

Whether it was the displeasure of Nehemiah or the ringing challenge of the prophet Malachi, the effect was immediate. We read, *"All Judah brought the tithes of grain, new wine and oil into the storerooms"* (Neh. 13:12). Reading between the lines, it seems that the people's response was most generous. So much so, that Nehemiah had to establish a three-man team of trustworthy individuals to oversee the collection and distribution of the supplies being brought in. Here are some of the details: *"I put Shelemiah the priest, Zadok the scribe, and a Levite named Pedaiah in charge of the storerooms and made Hanan son of Zaccur, the son of Mattaniah, their assistant, because these men were considered trustworthy. They were made responsible for distributing the supplies to their brothers"* (Neh. 13:13). Not only so but judging from the words of verse 15, God, in keeping with his promise through Malachi, sent an abundant harvest of grapes, grain, fruit and other commodities (cf. Mal. 3:10-11). There can be no doubt that when God's people are spiritually revived, they will be generous in their giving. The desperate measures resorted to by some modern, Christian fund-raisers is as much a testimony to the spiritual state of the Church as it is to that of the fund raisers themselves!

Anyone interested in researching the relationship between church renewal, personal devotion and Christian generosity should read Malachi 3 alongside 2 Corinthians chapters 8 and 9. There is no limit to what God will do when his people make room for Him to work and show themselves willing. Here are a couple of other scriptures that support Nehemiah's experience.

> *"Now who is willing to consecrate himself today to the Lord? Then the leaders of families, the officers of the tribes of Israel, the commanders of thousands, and the commanders of hundreds, and the officials in charge of the king's work gave willingly"* (1 Chron. 29:5b- 6).

> *"All the Israelites men and women who were willing brought to the Lord freewill offerings for all the work the Lord through Moses had commanded them to do…*

> *"…And the people continued to bring freewill offerings morning after morning. So all the skilled craftsmen who were doing all the work on the sanctuary left their work and said to Moses, 'The people are bringing more than enough for doing the work the Lord commanded to be done.' Then Moses gave an order and they sent this word throughout the camp: 'No man or woman is to make anything else as an offering for the sanctuary.'*

"And so the people were restrained from bringing more because what they already had was more than enough to do all the work" (Ex. 35:29 & 36:3b-7 — cf. Psalm 110:3).

4. Lessons for Today

Once again we see how much Nehemiah's efforts coupled with Malachi's challenging words can teach us. Both men point the way to spiritual renewal in any generation. It would appear that a number of today's churches are languishing either because of complicity with the world and its lifestyles, or because of the parsimony of their members.

We need a Nehemiah-style "clean-up bee" not only in our lives and homes but also in our fellowships. There is no question that missionary service is hindered, the Lord's work is stymied and millions are literally and spiritually starving for the "bread of life," while Christians live in comfort and luxury.

Do you remember the response of Uriah the Hittite when King David encouraged him to take time off from his military duties to relax at his home with his wife? This is what Uriah said, *"The ark and Israel and Judah are staying in tents, and my commander Joab and my lord's men are camped in the open country. How could I go to my house to eat and drink?"* (cf. 2 Sam. 11:11).

He certainly sounds like a man after Nehemiah's own heart (cf. also Haggai 1:2-4).

We need to heed the solemn warning of the prophet Malachi if we really want the Lord to visit us in blessing. Are we truly anxious for a visitation of God upon our lives and congregations? Then let us listen again to these solemn words of the prophet.

"'See, I will send my messenger, who will prepare the way before me. Then suddenly the Lord you are seeking will come to his temple; the messenger of the covenant, whom you desire, will come,' says the Lord Almighty. 'But who can endure the day of his coming? Who can stand when he appears. For he will be like a refiner's fire or a launderer's soap...

"So I will come to put you on trial. I will be quick to test-ify against sorcerers, adulterers, and perjurers, against those who defraud labourers of their wages, who oppress the widows and the fatherless, and deprive the foreigners among you of justice, but do not fear me,' says the Lord Almighty." (Mal. 3:1-5).

The question remains for us. Are we willing to toss out Tobiah's 'stuff' and bring the tithes into the storehouse?

CHAPTER NINE
MESSING WITH THE
MIXED MULTITUDE

"In those days I saw men in Judah treading winepresses on the Sabbath and bringing in grain and loading it on donkeys, together with wine, grapes, figs and all other kinds of loads. And they were bringing all this into Jerusalem on the Sabbath. Therefore I warned them against selling food on that day. Men from Tyre who lived in Jerusalem were bringing in fish and all kinds of merchandise and selling them in Jerusalem on the Sabbath to the people of Judah".

Nehemiah 13:15-16

1. Problem

How quickly people forget! On the completion of the wall, in the month Elul, 442 B.C, the returning exiles assembled in the square near the Water Gate to listen to Ezra the scribe reading aloud from the Book of the Law. The effect was dramatic. We read,

> *"On the twenty-fourth day of the same month, the Israelites gathered together, fasting and wearing sackcloth and having dust on their heads. Those of Israelite descent had separated themselves from all foreigners. They stood in their places and confessed their sins and the wickedness of their fathers. They stood where they were and read from the Book of the Law of the Lord their God for a quarter of the day, and spent another quarter in confession and in worshipping the Lord their God"* (Neh. 9:1-3).

Reading through Nehemiah chapter nine we discover that a number of different things happened after they had listened to the reading of the sacred Torah. There was not only a public, national confession of sin but a solemn commitment to obey the Word of the Lord. This was not simply a matter of 'lip service' nor a 'gentleman's agreement' but a solemn undertaking, a written and sealed, covenant document. In it the people, through their leaders, pledged themselves to undertake a number of responsibilities. These included a promise not to marry or allow their children to marry non Jews; a commitment to observe the Sabbath and a further pledge to fully support and maintain the service of the Lord's sanctuary (cf. Neh. 9:38-10:39).

Now, only twelve years later, following Nehemiah's brief absence from Jerusalem, what do we find? The Temple had practically fallen into disuse, except as a haven for the enemy. The Sabbath had been totally secularized and people were treating it as just another business day. Even as Nehemiah stepped in and attempted to put things right, he was met with a great reluctance to comply with his demands (cf. 13:15-22).

As if this were not enough, he found out that far from maintaining their racial purity as they had promised, the Jews had deliberately and consistently married wives from Philistia, Ammon and Moab—nations notorious for their hatred of Israel and her God. Nehemiah also found out that the offspring of these proscribed marriages were unable even to speak the Jews' language. This situation especially incensed him. Furthermore, it was not just the ordinary people who had despised and broken the covenant but their leaders and priests as well, including the son of Eliashib the high priest.

2. Reaction

This tragic state of affairs called for drastic action and Nehemiah was the man for the hour. We have already seen how he unceremoniously threw Tobiah's furniture out of the Temple and reinstated the Levites in their places. He now takes on the "nobles of Judah" and tells them in no uncertain terms to stop desecrating the Sabbath. Next, he stations his own men at strategic points to ensure that the city gates are closed on the Sabbath day and all trading stopped forthwith. We note one particularly amusing incident. Nehemiah discovers that traders and merchants who were reluctant to accept these Sabbath regulations, were camping and setting up shop just outside the city gates. Undaunted by their menacing attitudes, Nehemiah boldly challenges them and tells them to get lost!

This is how he describes what happened. *"But I warned them and said, 'Why do you spend the night by the wall? If you do this again, I will lay hands on you'"* (Neh. 13:21). They evidently got the message! (v. 22). In the case of the mixed marriages and "illiterate offspring" Nehemiah was even more forceful. He not only rebuked the miscreants, calling curses down on their heads, but he beat some of the men and pulled out their hair! Then he made them take an oath in God's name that they would desist from their evil practices (cf. 13:23-27). In a final flourish, he drove Eliashib's son, Joiada, out of office and purified the ceremonially defiled priests and Levites.

In passing, it is interesting to note the difference between the personalities and reactions of Nehemiah and Ezra when faced with similar situations. While Ezra pulled out his own hair, Nehemiah pulled out other people's! Both methods were evidently effective (cf. Ezra 9:3).

3. Result

Since the book of Nehemiah ends at this point we do not know what the lasting results of Nehemiah's actions were. All we know is that he at least felt satisfied that he had done the job as it needed to be done. As the book ends we hear Nehemiah say,

> *"So I purified the priests and the Levites of everything for-eign, and assigned them duties, each to his own task. I also made provision for contributions of wood at desig-nated times, and for the firstfruits.*
>
> *"Remember me with favour, O my God"* (Neh. 13:30-31).

4. Lessons for Today

Whatever we may think of Nehemiah's muscular Christianity, as we might describe it, it certainly was effective. He surely teaches us—methods apart—that there can be no cohabiting or compromise with evil if the work of the Lord is to prosper. Similarly, while we may not choose to defend Nehemiah's brand of Sabbath-keeping as necessarily Christian, the message is clear. Once we have made a commitment to live by what we regard as God's standards and rules, woe betide us if we go back on our word! Although as instructed believers we know and understand Christian ethics, unfortunately many of us still choose to "sail as near to the wind" as possible, spiritually speaking. We know God's wishes and warnings yet we conveniently choose to neglect them. Is it any wonder so many of our churches are spiritually weak and ineffective?

While the regulations regarding inter-racial marriages have little or no bearing on our domestic arrangements today since we are not members of that beleaguered Jewish community in Jerusalem, there are important moral and spiritual principles here from which we can learn. Scripture makes it clear that whether condoned in ancient Israel or among the Lord's people today, the "mixed multitude" ("rabble" NIV),is always a hindrance to progress and blessing (cf. Num. 11:4; 25:1-3). Welcoming unbelievers, however attractive, into the membership of a Christian church is to court disaster.

Obviously we must not attempt to play the role of judge nor be ungracious. However, we do non-Christians, not to mention the local church, a great disservice when we water down "the faith once delivered to the saints" in order to accommodate unbelievers. A credible confession of faith and manner of life must not be dismissed as unimportant. True spiritual separation, properly understood, is still vital to a church's survival.

Paul's command and his questions are still valid as in the early days of the Church. His point is precisely the same as Nehemiah's. *"Do not be yoked together with unbelievers. For what do righteousness and wickedness have in common? Or what fellowship can light have with darkness? What harmony is there between*

Christ and Belial? What does a believer have in common with an unbeliever?" (2 Cor. 6:14-15).

Of course, having recognized that important principle, we must be very careful to keep two other things in mind here. First, while Christians are called to separation from evil, they are not called to unfriendly separatism. That would negate the Great Commission. We cannot properly represent the *"friend of sinners"* by refusing to have anything to do with non Christians. A monastery may be a great place for meditation; it is a most unlikely place for evangelism!

Second, we must reject out of hand any suggestion that we separate ourselves from other true believers in Christ. We may not subscribe to some of their doctrinal emphases nor do things in the same way, but we must not despise brothers and sisters in Christ. Paul reminds us that it is absolutely contrary to the Word and Spirit of the Lord to refuse to fellowship with those whom Christ has received. Here are his words,

> *"Accept him whose faith is weak, without passing judgment on disputable matters." And again, "Accept one another, then, just as Christ accepted you, in order to bring praise to God."*
>
> *"I commend to you our sister Phoebe, a servant of the church in Cenchrea. I ask you to receive her in the Lord in a way worthy of the saints and to give her any help she may need from you, for she has been a great help to many people, including me"* (Rom. 14:1; 15:7 & 16:1-2).

We may sometimes feel a bit like Nehemiah and be tempted to pull a few beards and tear out a few hairs. However, before doing so we will be well advised to take a good long look in the mirror and ask ourselves whether we should start on the person we see there.

Certainly we could do with a few Nehemiah's around today. Hopefully they would be the kind of people who would have a measure of the temperament of Barnabas mixed in with that of Nehemiah! (Acts 11:24). That there is need for cleansing and true consecration in our lives, homes and local churches, is undeniable. However, let us remember the Pauline criteria before we go crusading. He writes: *"Brothers, if someone is caught in a sin, you who are spiritual should restore him gently. But watch yourself, or you also may be tempted"* (Gal. 6:1).

PART II

GOD AT WORK THROUGH PEOPLE

"'See, I will send my messenger, who will prepare the way before me. Then suddenly the Lord you are seeking will come to his temple; the messenger of the covenant, whom you desire, will come' says the Lord *Almighty".* Malachi 3:1

CHAPTER TEN
NEHEMIAH:
THE LEADER GOD USES

Despite his important role in Israel's history, we know few details about Nehemiah's personal life. He was evidently a member of a prominent Jewish family that had been transplanted from Jerusalem to Babylon in the days of Nebuchadnezzar. Judging from the fact that his own, his father's and his mother's names all included reference to the name of God, Nehemiah's family must have remained loyal in their worship of Jehovah during the long years of captivity. It is noteworthy that his brother Hanani became the spokesman for the beleaguered Jerusalem community. Indeed, the Elephantine papyri refer to a certain Hananiah being in charge of Jerusalem. This may well be the same person we know as Nehemiah's brother—(cf. NIV footnote on Neh. 7:2).

Under Persian rule Nehemiah himself achieved the distinction of being a member of King Artaxerxes the First's cupbearer corps. As we already recognized, such a privilege was granted to only the most trustworthy among the royal courtiers. A cupbearer was not simply a glorified butler or bartender; he was a confidant of the King and a member of the political inner circle.

Later of course, Nehemiah rose to be the King's appointee as governor of Judah. It was while holding this office that he achieved fame as the man who organized and accomplished the rebuilding of the walls of Jerusalem and the spiritual renewal of the city's Jewish community—(Neh. 5:14). Indications are that Nehemiah served as governor of Judea for twelve years, with one short absence from Jerusalem toward the end of his term in office. Evidently his brother Hanani deputized for him in his absence (7:2). In any case it is obvious that Nehemiah was an outstanding man in his nation. We do not know whether he was married nor whether he had his own family. This information being absent may suggest that he was celibate, perhaps even a eunuch, thus permitting him to serve in the royal harem and palace. This of course is only conjecture.

Characteristics

1. Personal Integrity

As we have already observed, Nehemiah was a man of personal integrity and honour to whom the shouldering of responsibility came naturally. It is also obvious that he had considerable administrative skills which he exercised as governor of Jerusalem. He knew how to allocate work, how to motivate people and he was not afraid to delegate responsibility to others. Chapter seven gives us a clear picture of Nehemiah's careful record keeping as well as his honest book-keeping. He mentions not only the names of those who contributed but includes the amounts of money and other gifts they gave to support the work. In passing, we discover that the number of the returned exiles, including servants and others, amounted to around 50,000 people. This gives us an idea of Nehemiah's administrative skill and leadership capabilities.

Here is the introductory statement from Nehemiah's own inventory:

> "Now the city was large and spacious, and there were few people in it, and the houses had not yet been rebuilt. So my God put it into my heart to assemble the nobles, the officials and the common people for registration by families. I found the genealogical record of those who had been the first to return. This is what I found written there…" (Neh. 7:4-5).

One section of this inventory is particularly interesting and shows how careful Nehemiah was to comply with the ancient ceremonial laws regarding inheritances and in particular, how he protected the purity of the priesthood. The following phrase is worth noting, "And from among the priests… These searched for their family records but they could not find them and so were excluded *from the priesthood as unclean. The governor, therefore, ordered them not to eat any of the most sacred food until there should be a priest ministering with the Urim and Thummim"* (Neh. 7:63-65). Presumably, such a person would be able to give a ruling in the matter based on his discernment of God's will, as revealed to him by means of the Urim and Thummim (cf. Ex. 28:30).

2. A Man of Discernment

As a leader, Nehemiah was discerning, a good judge of character. He not only exposed disloyalty on the part of pretenders (6:8-10) but appreciated loyalty and honesty in fellow workers and friends (Neh. 3:20; 7:2; 8:4; 12:25-26). Nehemiah not only directed people to work but inspired them to work by his own dedication and example. He was personally involved in the wall building project. Not only that, but he was prepared to soil his hands if need be. Clearly he served with commitment and enthusiasm (4:19-23).

3. A Careful Administrator

Nehemiah was also a good military strategist and a man of action. He recognized the importance of a careful reconnoitre and evidently believed, like any good Boy Scout, in being prepared. Although he was aware of the strength and determination of his enemies, he was not over-awed by that knowledge. Because of his personal confidence in God and his courage, he was able to inspire his men to stand firm in the defence of their city and nation.

4. A Good Strategist

Nehemiah was not militaristic in the sense of being aggressive and belligerent, but by the same token he was not easily intimidated. He recognized the strategic importance of building the walls and hanging up the gates of Jerusalem, and he also pursued operations in a careful and effective fashion. His defence plan was to deploy his forces as widely as possible in order to gain maximum cover, but he was careful not to spread them too thinly.

5. A Smart Psychologist

Nehemiah's campaign plan showed him to be a man who understood men. He decided that, rather than building one section of the city wall at a time, he would order the builders to work on the entire wall. Thus the project was to be carried forward up to the half way point (Neh. 4:6). While this meant that every part of the city remained equally vulnerable to enemy attack, it also meant that the builders would feel equally cared for by their leaders. Each group could see something happening. They would thus be inspired to build in a spirit of friendly competition, each getting on with his part of the job. Nehemiah recognized that when people see things being accomplished, they are motivated to press forward.

Another key feature of Nehemiah's strategy was his positioning of his troops and builders in the immediate environs of their own homes. This of course gave the men added incentive to work and stay alert. Each man would feel he had a vested interest in the project.

6. A Man of Determination

Beside his careful allocation of tasks and his call for the total involvement of people from every social stratum and walk in life, Nehemiah insisted that people accept dual roles. In addition to the regular guards, every builder was also armed and ready in case of surprise attack. Despite the inconvenience of having a weapon dangling at his side while trying to scale and build the wall, each man was sharply reminded of the imminent danger. Being fore-warned and fore-armed paid off.

Nehemiah's strategy has served the modern nation of Israel well in its continuing, precarious position among so many enemies. Although today's Israelis conduct their regular jobs and social activities fairly normally, they are all well trained soldiers and are ready at a moment's notice for that call to arms. The writer well remembers being guided around Israel by a civilian bus driver named Moses who just happened to double as a colonel in the Israeli army! It was reassuring, if a little disturbing, to realize that Moses' ordinary brief case held an Uzi machine gun. I realized that Nehemiah's "sword and travel" policy is still alive and well!

7. A Courageous Leader

We have already mentioned Nehemiah's courage. It certainly took courage to let his feelings show in the presence of King Artaxerxes and to request royal help to rebuild the walls of Jerusalem (2:1-5). It also took courage to resist the powerful, entrenched enemies who not only poured scorn on Nehemiah's project but threatened to harm him and his scattered work crew.

It was also courageous of him to expose and deal with the subversive elements among his own people, especially since some of them were highly placed and had considerable wealth and influence. Knowing his cause was just, Nehemiah was prepared to boldly face the odds no matter how they might be stacked against him.

8. A Generous Man

Another noteworthy trait in Nehemiah's character was his generosity. Although some of his fellow Jews might try to take advantage of any opportunity for financial profit, not so Nehemiah. He showed himself to be generous-hearted. For example, he not only declined to draw the salary allocated to him out of the royal purse, but fed and supported his entourage out of his own pocket (cf. 5:14-18).

Spiritual qualifications

1. A Man of Faith

Underlying all else was Nehemiah's commitment to his task as well as his complete trust in God. His was not a blind credulity but a genuine faith in God as his Sovereign, reliable, gracious Friend. It is clear that his own faith in God inspired others to believe with him. Here is a sample:

> "Then I said to them 'You see the trouble we are in: Jerusalem lies in ruins, and the gates have been burned

with fire. Come, let us rebuild the wall of Jerusalem and we will no longer be in disgrace. I also told them about the gracious hand of my God upon me and what the king had said to me.' They replied, 'Let us start rebuilding.' So they began this good work" (Neh. 2:17-18).

2. Man of Prayer

Nehemiah had an intelligent understanding of the Being and character of God. His theology undergirded his whole life and gave significance to any task, however mundane. He was a great believer in prayer. No matter what situation faced him, this leader instinctively prayed about it, and his prayer life was infectious.

3. Man of the Word

Another key element in Nehemiah's spiritual equipment was his knowledge and appreciation of the Word of God. His awareness of the great words of the Torah formed the basis of his prayer life. He reminded God of His promises and of His historic acts on behalf of Israel (1:8-10). When tempted by the enemy to compromise, it was Nehemiah's knowledge of priestly law that prevented his running to the Temple for refuge (6:10-12, see Num. 18:7).

His challenging of the people's failure in such matters as interracial marriages, the desecration of the Temple and the breakdown of the Sabbath stemmed from Nehemiah's understanding of Scripture. It was no doubt at Nehemiah's instigation that when the inhabitants of Jerusalem celebrated their first New Year in the city, everything was focussed on the prolonged reading and careful exposition of Scripture (8:1-3,8; 9: 3ff).

4. An Encourager

In New Testament terms, if there was one spiritual gift Nehemiah possessed above another, it was the gift of encouragement. Did people need help in face of enemy pressure? Were the builders discouraged by the seemingly endless mounds of rubbish? Had Israel lost its spiritual perspective in the matter of giving to support the Lord's work? Then Nehemiah was there to be the encourager!

Nehemiah was to the ancient community of the people of God in Jerusalem what a true shepherd or elder should be in a local church today. In fact, it would make an interesting study to list the qualifications for eldership prescribed in 1 Timothy 3:1-8 and Titus 1:3-8 and then see how they were exhibited in the life and ministry of Nehemiah.

Here then was the kind of man God used to bring about renewal and restoration among His people. There can be no question that, now as then, it is not a man's academic qualifications, nor his business acumen, nor his eloquence that fits him for Christian leadership—valuable though those things may be. It is his knowledge of God, his sense of mission and his willingness to serve without regard for financial reward or the praise of men.

CHAPTER ELEVEN
NEHEMIAH'S PRAYERS

It is not surprising that in a book which tells the story of spiritual return and renewal, such a strong emphasis should be placed on prayer. In fact, there are ten of Nehemiah's prayers recorded for us and each of them will repay careful study.

1. A Prayer of Confession 1:5-11

> "O Lord, God of heaven, the great and awesome God, who keeps his covenant of love with those who love him and obey his commands, let your ear be attentive and your eyes open to hear the prayer your servant is praying before you day and night for your servants, the people of Israel. I confess the sins we Israelites, including myself and my father's house, have committed against you. We have acted very wickedly toward you. We have not obeyed the commands, decrees and laws you gave your servant Moses" (1:5-7).

This first of Nehemiah's recorded prayers offers not only further insight into his character but also provides us with a helpful pattern for individual and corporate prayer. As we read through the prayer we shall see there are three important elements or emphases.

Adoration

The prayer begins with adoration and worship. There is an immediate recognition of the greatness and glorious majesty of God. This is evidenced in Nehemiah's use of no less than three of God's names or titles in quick succession. The first of these is Jehovah, a compound of the consonants from the Hebrew YHWH and the vowels from the title Adonai, regularly represented by LORD (upper case) in our English versions. This covenant name of God speaks not only of His eternity but also of His personal involvement in the affairs of His people.

The second name Nehemiah uses, *"God of Heaven"* (*elohe hashamayim*), reminds us of God's sovereignty and supremacy above all spiritual powers. It is reminiscent of the opening words of the Lord's prayer, *"Our Father in heaven"* (Matt. 6:9).

Nehemiah's third name or, more accurately, descriptive title for God, *"the great and awesome God,"* bespeaks His divine glory and holiness. It ties in with Nehemiah's later phrase, *"your servants who delight in revering your name"* (v. 11). He goes on to describe God as the one who *"keeps his covenant of love [chesed]."* This Hebrew word *chesed,* frequently translated "mercy," relates to God's unfailing kindness to those who are associated with him in a covenant of grace. Obviously, Nehemiah is counting heavily on the revealed character of God as he recognizes the great need of the hour.

Confession

One of the elements, as conspicuous by its presence in biblical prayers as by its absence in some of our contemporary prayers, is confession. Here, Nehemiah like Daniel, does not hesitate to identify himself and his family with the sin of the nation (Dan. 9:8-19). He is not simply trying to "twist God's arm" so to speak, but, true leader that he is, Nehemiah is sincerely penitent. He is honestly identifying himself with the spiritual and moral shortcomings of his people.

Petition (v. 5 & ll)

Several things become clear in Nehemiah's petition. First he recognizes the special relationship between God and Israel, noting they are *"your servants"* and *"your people whom you redeemed."* Second, he bases his requests and his confidence on the declared promise of God (v. 8-9). Third, he looks at life in true perspective. However unpredictable and capricious Artaxerxes the King may be, he is simply, in the idiom of prayer, "this man." Once again Nehemiah would have concurred with Daniel's world view, *"The Most High is sovereign over the kingdoms of men and gives them to anyone he wishes"* (Dan. 4:17). In passing, it is important to recognize how specific Nehemiah is in prayers. Instead of aiming at everything and hitting nothing, Nehemiah fires one "prayer bullet" at a time at a specific target. For example, we hear him asking God to give him favour with "this man," "today." No wonder his prayers were answered! (2:4).

2. An emergency prayer (2:4).

This brief petition, probably the most famous of Nehemiah's prayers, was absolutely spontaneous. Unlike his first recorded prayer, there is no pattern or order about it. In fact, we do not know the content of the prayer; we can only conjecture.

Faced with a crisis—indeed what might have been a life-or-death situation, Nehemiah reacts instinctively. There was no time to think, no place to hide; it was now or never. His simple sentence spells it out so beautifully, *"Then I prayed to the God of heaven and I answered the king."*

Such straightforward simplicity suggests intimacy with God. Nehemiah was as familiar with the court of Heaven as he was with the court of Artaxerxes. In fact, he realized that his God was much more accessible than the king. It was this that gave Nehemiah his courage and decisiveness.

We can learn several lessons from this prayer. First, it bespeaks a life of prayer, reminding us of the importance of cultivating a habit of prayer. It was, we might say, "second nature" for Nehemiah to consult God about everything.

Second, the prayer displays confidence in God. Had Nehemiah been wavering and vacillating as he nervously approached the king, he might have blurted out some quite inappropriate answer. As it was, because of his calm confidence in the Lord, his split-second prayer and guarded response saved the day both for himself and his nation.

Third, we learn that when it comes to prayer, what matters is not, long-windedness, nor even brevity, but reality. That Nehemiah's prayer was heard and answered is again quite obvious from its far-reaching results.

3. Imprecatory prayers.

> *"Hear us, O our God, for we are despised. Turn their insults back on their own heads. Give them over as plunder in a land of captivity. Do not cover up their guilt or blot out their sins from your sight, for they have thrown insults in the face of the builders"* (4:4-5).

> *"Remember Tobiah and Sanballat, O my God, because of what they have done; remember also the prophets Noadiah and the rest of the prophets who have been trying to intimidate me"* (6:14, see also 13:29).

These prayers sound a bit unusual by Christian standards but are perfectly natural and acceptable if understood against the wider context of Nehemiah's theology. At first sight, the imprecatory prayers of the Old Testament seem rather inappropriate. They appear to reflect a vindictive spirit, if not a raw desire for revenge. And of course, if that was the prayer's intent, such prayers would be unworthy.

However, generally speaking, if we examine the life-context out of which such prayers grew, while obviously personal emotions are involved, imprecatory prayers tend to be cries for God to demonstrate his righteousness. As in the petitions we are looking at, the suppliant is expressing his frustration and saying to God in so many words, 'O God I am in trouble; as far as I can tell, my cause is your cause. Please demonstrate your righteous indignation against these enemies of yours and mine! Show them that sin against You does not ultimately go unpunished.'

We see that Nehemiah's problem here was the ridicule and intrigue of Tobiah and Sanballat (Neh. 4:1-3& 6:14). Certainly these characters were opposed to Nehemiah, but he had incurred their hatred, not because of something personal, but because of the position he held as leader of the people of Israel. It was not a question of personal vendetta therefore. These men hated anyone and everyone who got in their way. Ultimately, their animosity and stratagems were directed against the Lord, as much as against Nehemiah. Seen in this light we can better appreciate Nehemiah's words.

The third imprecatory prayer found in Nehemiah 13:29 is certainly lacking in any feeling or desire for personal revenge. Nehemiah was righteously indignant at the scandalous behaviour of some of the priests, including members of the high priest's own family. He sensed that there was a particular seriousness about what he considered to be a blatant contravention of God's Law on the part of these leaders. If the priests were wrong, what hope was there for the people? It was with this in mind that Nehemiah prays, *"Remember them, O my God, because they have defiled the priestly office and the covenant of the priesthood and of the Levites."*

Of course having said that, let us face it, Nehemiah was not perfect, nor ever pretended to be. If we detect some degree of personal animosity toward Tobiah and Sanballat, who could blame him? Which of us has never experienced similar feelings? The very fact that the Bible faithfully records Nehemiah's words is an indication of its frankness.

4. Prayer plus!

"But we prayed to our God and posted a guard day and night to meet this threat" (4:9).

Someone has said, "We Christians should get busy and answer a lot of our own prayers!" Certainly there is a measure of truth in that. How often we lazily ask God to do things for us that we could very well do ourselves! For example, in our evangelism we pray that God will send people in to hear us preach the Gospel. How can we expect God to do for us what he has already commissioned us to do?—that is to *"go into all the world"* (Mark 16:15) as His heralds!

It's a bit like our doing something foolish and then asking God to help us get out of our scrapes! Obviously, we are not denying the fact that God very graciously will come to our aid, despite our foolishness. He is boundlessly merciful and often saves us from ourselves. However, we ought not to presume on divine grace.

Nehemiah had the right idea. He prayed and then he took precautions. He realized that there are some things that only God can do and for those we depend on him utterly. On the other hand there are some things we must do for ourselves. These we must do in the strength that God supplies. Perhaps the order here is significant too. Notice it was prayer first, action second.

Do you find yourself making elaborate plans, then asking for God's approval and help. Surely we would be well advised to pray and seek the Lord's direction before we make our plans or act precipitously. Having sought to discover God's will, we can then watch and pray and await His direction. Of course, the scriptural exhortation is to *"pray without ceasing"* — certainly a tall order (1 Thess. 5:17).

5. Personal Prayers

> *"Remember me with favour, O my God, for all I have done for these people"* (Neh. 5:19).

> *"But I prayed, 'Now strengthen my hands'"* (Neh. 6:9b).

> *"Remember me for this, O my God, and do not blot out what I have so faithfully done for the house of my God and its services"* (Neh. 13:14).

> *"Remember me with favour, O my God"* (Neh. 13:31).

These four personal prayers surely sound a bit strange to our ears. They seem like the proverbial: "God bless me and my wife; my son and his wife, us four and no more!" However, we must be careful not to misunderstand. There may be several explanations. One may be that Nehemiah was a rather sensitive, artistic person of melancholic temperament. Such people are capable of great achievements but they also are inclined to feel threatened when criticized. They may even become withdrawn, feeling misunderstood or even lonely and depressed. Such folk have a real need for reinforcement and encouragement. Could it be that sensing the loneliness that accompanies leadership and pressed by the clamant needs of the people and the project, Nehemiah bared his heart and just threw himself on God?

Another explanation may be that the book of Nehemiah is largely composed of Nehemiah's personal memoirs and diary entries. Often people record private and personal thoughts and prayers in their diaries, none of which is intended for publication. Some people even write to their diary! If we are honest, most of us have experienced those private moments when we have prayed words similar to these personal prayers of Nehemiah. Have you known times when you've been a bit down and felt that only God understood?

Although a steady diet of such introspective devotion is not good for any of us, at least it suggests a sense of intimacy with God as our Friend, and that is surely commendable. At times, we can all identify with Jacob, Elijah, Jeremiah and Peter in their moments of stress. Life is not all smiles and success. Many Christians find themselves asking with David, *"Why are you downcast, O my soul? Why so disturbed within me?"* (Ps. 42:5,11) or, praying with Nehemiah, *"Remember me for this, O my God!"*

Prayer and promise (Neh. 9:5-38)

> *"Blessed be your glorious name, and may it be exalted above all blessing and praise. You alone are the* LORD. *You made the heavens, even the highest heavens, and all their starry host, the earth and all that is on it, the seas and all that is in them. You give life to everything, and the multitudes of heaven worship you"* (Neh. 9: 5-6).

It is not surprising that the longest prayer in the Book of Nehemiah is associated with a time of national repentance and renewal, encouraged by the Word of God. The occasion was a sort of national, spiritual retreat. First, there was mourning for and confession of sin; second, a commitment to a path of separation from evil; third, a very lengthy public reading of the Word of God and finally, a time of national worship. No wonder we read, as a sequel to all this, *"And the Levites… said:*

'Stand up and praise the Lord your God who is from everlasting to everlasting'" (v. 5).

There follows quite naturally from this point, a fairly lengthy prayer. Its elements are:

   i. An appreciation of the greatness of God (v. 5-6);
  ii. A recitation of the goodness of God during Israel's long history (v. 7-15; 19-25; 32-35);
 iii. An admission of national guilt because of disobedience and idolatry (v. 16-18; 26-31);
 iv. A confession of present need (v. 36-37)

Some parts of the prayer sound like a recapitulation of the events described in the Book of Judges (Judg. 2:16-19).

This prayer is followed by the drawing up of a covenant in which the people and their leaders as cosignatories promise to do a number of things. These include: refusing to inter-marry with non Jews; honouring the Sabbath; payment of tithes and offerings and care of the House of God. It all sounds very promising, but unfortunately, judging from subsequent events, it was "honoured more in its breach than its observance."

These then are the prayers of the Book of Nehemiah. Few national leaders, even in Israel's illustrious history, have been more committed to prayer or more effective in their accomplishments than Nehemiah. He was neither a priest nor an official religious leader. His office was secular but he had a clear understanding of what makes a nation truly great. His life is an illustration of the words of James, *"The prayer of a righteous man is powerful and effective"* (Jas. 5:16). The prayers of this righteous man were powerful!

CHAPTER TWELVE
THE GOD NEHEMIAH WORSHIPED

There is sometimes the danger that when we read the narrative parts of Scripture we merely focus on the history rather than theology - not that they can ultimately be divorced from each other. After all, the Bible is a book about God. It begins and ends with God speaking and revealing Himself. Evangelicals believe that since all Scripture is inspired, when it speaks, God speaks. Therefore, whether anything is actually stated about God, that is, in the precise terms of systematic theology, there is always something of His character and glory being revealed. Even in the book of Esther where the name of God is not even mentioned, His presence, purpose and power are everywhere manifest. Thus it is that, as we read through the Book of Nehemiah, we discern the ways and working of Nehemiah's God. Whether in the Persian court in Susa or among the mounds of rubbish in Jerusalem, God is there. Whether through the decree of a despotic Artaxerxes, the calumny of a cynical Sanballat, or the disloyalty of a vacillating Eliashib, God's purposes will be accomplished!

Quite apart from its implied theology, the Book of Nehemiah is full of plain statements about the character and attributes of God. We will take a brief look at them in the following paragraphs.

1. The Eternity of God.

As the Levites exhort the people to publicly confess their national sin they say, *"Stand up and praise the Lord your God, who is from everlasting to everlasting"* (9:5). What follows is a brief resumé of Israel's history. The Levites' point seems to be that while God's ways are manifest in time, He "inhabits eternity."

2. "God is Spirit"

Although the full disclosure of the truth of God's spiritual nature must await New Testament revelation, it is already suggested in the Old Testament. In fact, it is here in the same great prayer of the Levites that we hear them say, *"You gave your good Spirit to instruct them"* (9:20). They continue, *"By your Spirit you admonished them through your prophets"* (v. 30). Two things become clear from these words. One is that God's gracious Spirit cared for His people, the other is that the Spirit is the one who inspired the prophets both in their oral and written ministry.

3. God's Personality

Despite the Old Testament writers' emphasis on the transcendence and greatness of God, they are very aware of his personal immanence. This is so evident in the Book of Nehemiah. For example, Nehemiah quotes God speaking in the first person singular, *"I will scatter you among the nations... I will gather them... I have chosen as a dwelling for my Name"* (1:8-9).

Then note Nehemiah's intimate description of God as *"my God."* He says *"the gracious hand of my God was upon me"* (2:8). This is not just "the typical anthropomorphism of primitive theism," as the critics claim. It is Nehemiah's realization of God's personal care and superintendence (cf. 2:12; 4:20; 6:16; 7:5.; 9:3; 10:32,34).

Linked with this revelation of the personality of God is, "the Name." In the verse cited above, we have God saying, *"I will gather them from there and bring them to the place I have chosen as a dwelling for my Name"* (1:9).

The name in Scripture is not just a means of identification but a revelation of personal character. In fact, the especially personal name Yahweh or LORD is used seventeen times in the thirteen chapters of Nehemiah.

Further confirmation of God's Personal Being is offered in the many references to His answering the prayers of His children. We hear Nehemiah saying, *"Let your ear be attentive and your eyes open to hear the prayer your servant is praying before you day and night"* (1:6. See also 1:11, 2:4; 4:4; 6:9,14; 13:14,22,29,31). There can be no question that, as far as Nehemiah is concerned, God is personal and near.

4. God's Greatness

It is clear, right from his earliest references to God in the book, that Nehemiah had an appreciation of the greatness and power of God. Four times he refers to *"the God of heaven"* (1:4-5; 2:4,20). He begins his first recorded prayer with the words, *"O Lord, God of Heaven, the great and awesome God,"* and concludes with a reference to God's *"great strength and your mighty hand"* (1:5,10).

Nehemiah sees God's power revealed both in creation and in His providence. We hear him say, *"You alone are the Lord. You made the heavens, even the highest heavens, and all their starry host, the earth and all that is on it, the seas and all that is in them. You give life to everything, and the multitudes of heaven worship you"* (9:6).

It is clear from this final sentence that God is recognized as being worshiped in the celestial realms as well as on the earth (cf. 5:13 and 9:5). Other verses that speak of God's greatness and creatorial might include 8:6; 9:6,10,21 and 32.

5. God's Sovereignty.

Nehemiah sees God's sovereignty as a further demonstration of His Greatness. He acknowledges that it is through God's over-ruling that he not only gains access and favour with King Artaxerxes (1:11; 2:1), but is given authority and provisions for the success of his mission to Jerusalem (2:18, 20).

When the enemy attempts to hinder the work, it is God who frustrates his evil designs (4:15). Then, when Shemaiah tries to inveigle Nehemiah into an illegal rendezvous in the Temple, it is God who makes Nehemiah realize he is about to walk into a trap (6:12).

The long prayer of the Levites in chapter 9 is full of statements about the sovereignty of God. He chooses Abram; delivers Israel from Egypt; gives them the Law and provides for them in their desert trek. He gives them the land of Canaan, displacing other nations to do so, and all this despite their rebellion and ingratitude (9:7-28).

The Attributes of God

It is sometimes difficult for us to distinguish between the attributes and the character of God. They are like the two sides of one coin. However, for the sake of getting a clearer picture we will look at such divine attributes as Holiness, Grace and the Saving Love of God.

Holiness

While there is no definitive statement in the Book of Nehemiah such as, *"Holy is the Lord"* — the idea of God's holiness is constantly present. In this book the emphasis is not so much on God's ceremonial holiness as on His moral holiness, not just God's separateness from sin as "The Holy Other," but His demand for holiness in the lives of those who claim to be His worshipers. God's Righteousness, which of course is the expression of His holiness, requires righteousness in His people (8:8).

There is no question that God is to be revered and obeyed (cf. 1:11; 5:15; 7:2). Furthermore, to disobey and rebel is to court disaster. God is holy, and since sin in any form is an affront to his holiness, it must be punished. This is true even in the case of the heathen (4:5). Of course it was Israel's idolatry and sin against the Lord that brought about the Exile and the sad condition of Jerusalem as Nehemiah found it.

God had used Gentile nations to destroy the city and take His people into captivity (1:7-8; 9:27,28). This idea is poignantly expressed in the great Levitical prayer, *"In all that has happened to us, you have been just; you have acted faithfully, while we did wrong"* (9:33).

God's holiness, or separateness from sin, is to be reflected in the lives of those who claim to be His. For example, the exploitation of fellow Jews is wrong because it is a denial of God's holiness or moral standard (5:9 and 5:15). Hanani's dual qualifications for responsibility were his integrity and his fear of God (7:2).

Nehemiah's quarrel with the Sabbath breakers was not simply that it was a contravention of Israel's ceremonial arrangements. It was a desecration of God's special or holy day (see 8:9,10; 13:15ff). Similarly, his complaint against Eliashib the High Priest was that he had committed sacrilege by allowing Tobiah to set himself up in the Temple, a place which was set apart for the LORD (13:7-10, 6:10).

It is in this same light that we are to understand the prohibition of mixed marriages. Israel was God's special people. They were separate (holy) from other nations as His chosen ones. For them to intermarry with people who were in rebellion against God was tantamount to denying God's holiness - at least in its practical, daily application (Neh. 10:30, 13:23ff.).

Two other matters reflect Nehemiah's belief in the holiness of God. One is the recognition of the need for confession and repentance. Sin, which is always a challenge of the holiness of God, must be confessed and dealt with (1:6-7; 9:1-2). The other matter is the necessity for purification. While this was part of the ceremonial culture, it was also a recognition that God's holiness requires a commitment to purity on the part of his servants (12:30, 45).

Grace

There are numerous references to God's Grace in the Book of Nehemiah. Here is a sample. In 2:8 and 18 Nehemiah speaks of, *"the gracious hand of my God was upon me."* Then in the great prayer of Chapter 9 we read, *"But you are a forgiving God, gracious and compassionate, slow to anger and abounding in love,"* (v. 17, see v. 19, 27, 28, 31, 35).

Quite apart from these specific references, God's Grace is one of the underlying motifs of the book. Two other truths are related to this theme of divine grace. They are God's revelation of Himself and His covenant-keeping. We might also include His willingness to answer prayer. However, we have already dealt with that in connection with God's personality.

God graciously reveals Himself personally to individuals. For example, we hear Nehemiah saying, *"I had not told anyone what my God had put in my heart to do for Jerusalem"* (Neh. 2:12). This is repeated in Nehemiah 7:5, *"So my God put it into my heart to assemble the nobles, the officials and the common people for registration by families."*

God also reveals himself in his Word. As Nehemiah prays he says, *"Remember the instruction you gave your servant Moses, saying..."* (1:8).

In 8:1 reference is made to, *"the Book of the Law of Moses, which the Lord had commanded for Israel"* (see also v. 14). This idea of God's self-disclosure is made even more specific in 9:13 where we read, *"You came down on Mount Sinai; you spoke to them from Heaven. You gave them regulations and laws that are just and right, and decrees and commands that are good"* (see also Neh. 9:20 and 10:29).

God's covenant keeping, or faithfulness, is a further evidence of His grace. We hear Nehemiah praying, *"O Lord, God of heaven, the great and awesome God, who keeps his covenant of love with those who love him and obey his commands..."* (1:5).

Again this is in view in 9:7-8, *"You are the Lord God, who chose Abram and brought him out of Ur of the Chaldeans and named him Abraham. You found his heart faithful to you, and you made a covenant with him..."*

Saving Love

Although Nehemiah is fully aware of his nation's sin and of God's wrath against sin, he always counts on God's Salvation. For example, having confessed Israel's sin, he immediately goes on to say, *"They are your servants and your people, whom you redeemed by your great strength and your mighty hand"* (1:10). The particular redeeming act in view here is, of course, the Exodus.

We see the same sort of thing in the national prayer event. Israel's deliverances are all traced to God's saving grace (see Neh. 8:11,12, 15,17,24). We note especially the words of 9:27, *"From heaven you heard them, and in your great compassion you gave them deliverers, who rescued them from the hand of their enemies."*

Perhaps the clearest statement of all in this connection is heard in Nehemiah 9:17, *"But you are a forgiving God, gracious and compassionate, slow to anger and abounding in love."*

We see then that, for all its being a rather sad tale of broken walls and failing people, the Book of Nehemiah can teach us a great deal about the Glory and Character of God.

CHAPTER THIRTEEN
HALLMARKS OF
RENEWAL

In the existential climate of our day it is easy to be mistaken regarding the hallmarks of spiritual renewal. As the saying goes, "All that glitters is not gold." If you are looking for sterling, it is always wise to check for and identify the hallmarks. It is not enough to believe the promising sign outside the store, "Genuine antiques made and sold here." By the same token, it is unwise to judge the spiritual life and effectiveness of a church by its expensive building complex, its antiquity, traditional liturgies, music or entertaining programs. Show-biz techniques may attract crowds and generate excitement but they often amount to very little in the end. Church ads that promise to set you on the road to financial prosperity or that guarantee your health and well-being, while appealing, do not represent authentic, biblical Christianity.

In contrast to the fore-going, we can discover so much help and understanding about genuine spiritual renewal in this Book of Nehemiah. Although written as a descriptive narrative about a particular period in the history of the nation of Israel, this book is strikingly up to date both in its message and practical wisdom. "Rubbish removal" and "wall building" certainly do not sound very exciting or inspirational. Nevertheless, when God is directing and His people are willing, the most mundane jobs can take on the atmosphere of worship. In the following paragraphs we will consider seven hallmarks of spiritual renewal suggested in the story of Nehemiah.

1. Obedience to the Word of God

First, let us consider some of the relevant passages:

> "Remember the instruction you gave your servant Moses,
> saying, 'If you are unfaithful, I will scatter you among the

nations, but if you return to me and obey my commands,
then even if your exiled people are at the farthest horizon,
I will gather them from there and bring them to the place
I have chosen as a dwelling for my Name'" (Neh. 1:8-9;
see Lev. 26:33; Deut. 30:4).

They told Ezra the scribe to bring out the Book of the Law of Moses, which the Lord had commanded for Israel. Ezra the priest brought the Law before the assembly, which was made up of men and women and all who were able to understand. He read it from daybreak till noon as he faced the square before the Water Gate in the presence of the assembled people. And all the people listened attentively to the Book of the Law.

He read from the Book of the Law making it clear and giving the meaning so that the people could understand what was being read (cf. Neh. 8:2 - 8).

> *"All these now join their brothers the nobles, and bind*
> *themselves with a curse and an oath to follow the Law of*
> *God given through Moses the servant of God and to obey*
> *carefully all the commands, regulations and decrees of the*
> *Lord our Lord"* (10:29).

> *"On that day the Book of Moses was read aloud in the hear-*
> *ing of the people..."* (13:1).

It is clear from these passages from the Book of Nehemiah that the Word of God was of paramount importance in this time of Israel's restoration. God's Word gave them safe guidelines for all their decisions and actions. The question was not, "What would be expedient in this situation?" nor, "What do you feel about this, Nehemiah?" nor even, "How can we whip up some enthusiasm so that these people will give more money and work harder?" Rather it was, "What do the Scriptures say?" That may sound so basic, so obvious, or as we might say, "a no-brainer."

However, even among many so-called evangelical Christians today, the terms of reference are not necessarily the scriptures of truth. Often the criteria are things such as the latest pronouncements of some popular preacher, the latest directive from denominational headquarters, or what will keep our people happy?

It used to be that it was the liberals and modernists who offered alternatives to Scriptural truth and method. Now it is sometimes those who, while giving lip service to biblical inspiration, seem just as ready to follow the lure of experience or such doubtful phenomena as "exciting prophetic words for today!" Nehemiah might well have found it tempting to go that route. It would surely have been much more exhilarating than pushing wheel barrows full of rubbish and laying course upon course of bricks and stones. However, he chose to focus attention on the Word of the Lord.

We too will be well-advised to keep in mind the following word of the Lord recorded for us in the Book of Jeremiah:

> *"'I have heard what the prophets say who prophesy lies in my name. They say, 'I had a dream! I had a dream!' How long will this continue in the hearts of these lying proph-ets, who prophesy the delusions of their own minds? ... Let the prophet who has a dream tell his dream, but let the one who has my word speak it faithfully. For what has straw to do with grain?' declares the Lord"* (Jer. 23:25-28).

It is interesting to see the reaction of the people as Ezra read on and on from the pages of Scripture—they began to weep! It is worth noting that the careful, public reading of God's Word was not just part of the preliminaries—as it is often regarded in some contemporary Sunday morning Orders of Service. The reading of Scripture was the central item on the agenda! Certainly, the choir-singing and the praise came later and were important. However, the foundation of the worship, like the secret of renewal, was the reading, hearing and obey-ing of the Word of God.

We can also learn some practical lessons from this pro-longed public reading of Scripture. First, the Scriptures were read clearly and audibly. Second, we read, *"they gave the sense."* This underlines the importance of the careful exposition of Scripture. Personal testimony and storytelling have their place but there is no substitute for the systematic and well prepared exegesis of the biblical text.

2. A Commitment to Prayer

Nehemiah's prayer life is the subject of another chapter. Here, we see the effect of his teaching regarding prayer, as well as how his own example influenced the people he led. As we read through the prayer recorded in chapter nine several things surface. First, recognition is given to the sovereignty and power of God throughout Israel's history. Second, there is confession of persistent national failure. Third, and this seems remarkable, the prayer contains no direct request for help or for divine intervention. It is as though the people lay the whole sorry situation before God, make a clear commitment to rectify what is wrong, and then leave the rest to His grace. There is no attempt to pressure or plea bargain with God, just a willingness to wait on Him. It is reminiscent of the prayer in Tate and Brady's famous hymn.

> Let it come, O Lord we pray Thee,
> Let the shower of blessing fall:
> We are waiting, We are waiting
> Oh, revive the hearts of all.

Whatever lessons on prayer we can learn from Nehemiah and the people of God in Jerusalem, as well as from those times of renewal and revival in Christian history, it is clear that prevailing intercession on the part of Spirit-filled believers is effective. This very principle is of course clearly stated in the Lord's words to Solomon at the dedication of the first Temple, *"If my people, who are called by my name, will humble themselves and pray and seek my face and turn from their wicked ways, then I will hear from heaven and will forgive their sin and will heal their land"* (2 Chron. 7:14).

3. The Centrality of Worship

Another important lesson about renewal that we learn from the Book of Nehemiah is the importance of worship. This is especially significant when we recognize that it was Ezra the priest whose task was to rebuild the altar and the Temple (Ezra 3:3; 3:10ff). Nehemiah's job was to rebuild the walls of the city. However, he recognized that worship was not just something to be done on special occasions. He understood that essentially, it is an attitude of heart which controls all of life's activities, even the most mundane.

Of course, with the completion of the walls there was a particular feeling of elation among the people. It was at this point that the special wooden podium was set up so that Ezra could be seen by everyone, as he read from the Law of God. As always, the Word of God and worship go together. It was the recitation and exposition of Scripture that led to the rediscovery and celebration of the ancient Feast of Tabernacles. This is how it went,

> "On the second day of the month, the heads of all the families, along with the priests and the Levites, gathered around Ezra the scribe to give attention to the words of the Law. They found written in the Law, which the LORD had commanded through Moses, that the Israelites were to live in booths during the feast of the seventh month and that they should proclaim this word and spread it throughout their towns and in Jerusalem: 'Go out into the hill country and bring back branches from olive and wild olive trees, and from myrtles, palms and shade trees to make booths—as it is written.... The whole company that had returned from exile built booths and lived in them. From the days of Joshua son of Nun until that day, the Israelites had not celebrated it like this. And their joy was very great" (Neh. 8:13-17).

As we saw earlier, the people's initial response to hearing the Word of God was to mourn and weep. Now, having expressed their penitence, they are able to move forward to a time of joyous praise and worship. That, of course, is what is to be expected when the Lord's people are moved by God's Spirit and in a right attitude of heart.

This should certainly remind us that when, as believers, we

come together to celebrate the Lord's Supper, which of course is such an important element in any church's congregational worship, there is likely to be a mingling of sadness, as we recall the cost of our redemption, with joy as we remember Christ's glorious victory and coming again.

The Feast of Tabernacles was one of the three most important festivals in Israel's calendar, the other two being Passover and Pentecost. This feast had evidently been neglected during the time of the monarchy and the Exile. The only other record of its post-exilic celebration was in the time of Zerubbabel (cf. Ezra 3:4).

Now here, on this special occasion, Ezra had begun his public reading of the Book of the Law of the Lord on the first day of Tishri, ushering in the civic new year. By a happy coincidence, his reading uncovered the fact that the Feast of Tabernacles should be regularly celebrated from the fifteenth to the twenty first of that very month! Plans were therefore made immediately for the people to comply. They were to collect branches in order to build temporary booths. These shelters were built in commemoration of Israel's forty-year desert trek, subsequent to the Exodus.

The Feast of Tabernacles, or Succoth, to give it its Hebrew name, was essentially a time of happy commemoration of God's goodness to His people in their ancient desert journey and also thanksgiving for the fruit harvest. Judging from Nehemiah 8:18, this particular year it was a very significant and special time. For obvious reasons, it was a unique moment in Israel's national history calling for exuberant expressions of worship. The festival engendered a special sense of freedom and gratitude to God for his intervention on their behalf as well as His generous provision.

When people are renewed in their devotion to the Lord and are seeking to live in obedience to the Word of God, the tenor of their worship is likely to be lifted to new heights. In our contemporary scene, it is often possible to assess a church's spiritual life from the tenor of its worship. The styles and liturgies may vary but the important constants are the members' obedience to the Word and their appreciation of the Person and work of the Lord Jesus.

4. The Enjoyment of Unity

Another sign of spiritual renewal among God's people is unity of heart and purpose. This is so obviously present in our story, particularly as the wall was being built. We have already noticed that almost without exception, people of every rank and station pitched in to help the work go forward. Whether it was Eliashib and his fellow priests rebuilding the Sheep Gate or Malkijah the son of Rechab rebuilding the Dung Gate, no task was considered inconsequential. There was a wonderful sense of harmony and responsibility (cf. chapter 3). The same was true when the people assembled to hear the Word of God and to sing His praise. They assembled as one man, bound by common cause and commitment. It was not just a case of everyone trying to conform to prescribed traditions or doing what they were told. The people pursued their various tasks enthusiastically, recognizing that each person's task complemented that of all the others. Of course when discord arises, as in the case of the Tekoa nobles, troubles follow.

We cannot lay too much emphasis upon the importance and significance of unity among believers. According to Ephesians 4, unity is one of the evidences of the presence of an ungrieved Holy Spirit. This was a truth so dear to the heart of the Apostle Paul. He recognized, as did Nehemiah's wall builders all those years earlier, that unity is not a preferred option but an essential element in fruitful church fellowship. Of course, we shall be wise to recognize that unity is not uniformity, a fact so often overlooked. There was and is great opportunity for diversity of expression and understanding but we are still called *"to make every effort to maintain the unity of the Spirit in the bond of peace"* (Eph. 4:3). When the people of God are united it shows in at least two ways. There is joy in the Spirit and there is a gracious tolerance of differences of style. Incidentally, according to the Lord Jesus Himself, Christian unity offers an eloquent witness to an unbelieving world (John 17:20-23).

5. Separation from Sin

However noisy the celebration or however orthodox the language, there is no genuine renewal, be it personal or in churches, unless there is separation from sin. It may look easy to sweep sin under the rug and pretend that "everything in the garden is lovely" but God is not deceived and phoniness is quickly exposed. When true revival comes, consciences are disturbed and sin is dealt with. Indeed, it is quite moving to see people getting reconciled and making restitution. Many a local merchant has been grateful for the practical results of revival, even if he does not fully understand what is going on!

There are several instances of people making amends and straightening things out in Nehemiah's story. Initially there was some reluctance to comply but eventually things happened. For example, when Nehemiah discovered that the wealthy were exploiting the poor, he condemned it outright and gradually things were put right (5:1-12). Then, in the matter of inter-racial marriages, a particularly sensitive situation, it was only after loud remonstrances and threats that anything happened and people complied (13:23-27). Of course, in these situations Nehemiah's strong leadership was crucial. Had he compromised and accommodated the miscreants in any way, the blessing would have dried up. As it was, Nehemiah lowered the boom on priest and commoner alike. People accepted his direction, not only because of his forthrightness, but because they respected his personal example and integrity.

We have a particularly striking example of Nehemiah's courage and determination to rid the nation of evil as we see him tossing Tobiah's furniture out of the Temple. As people watched they probably gasped at Nehemiah's boldness in dealing with such a powerful enemy. However, come what may, let the chips fall where they will, Nehemiah was determined to root out sin. Little wonder there was blessing!

6. A Willingness to Work

A further hallmark of renewal seen in the Book of Nehemiah is the people's willingness to work or, perhaps a better word would be, to "serve" When Nehemiah and his people arrived in Jerusalem there was very little to appeal, certainly none of the comforts of home. If anything was to happen, the returned exiles had to make it happen. There were walls to be built, burdens to be carried and gates to be hung—quite apart from all the usual amenities required by families. Priests, farmers, artisans, merchants and professionals all worked together with a will. God's work needed to be done and, at this stage, that was all the incentive the people needed!

Today, we hear people saying things like, "that church has nothing to offer me," or "there's not much there for our family." It is as though people are looking for a country club that will cater to their every whim and wish. They prefer nice choirs, good music, splendid dinners, the best in entertainment, comfortable pews and of course, ear-tickling sermons. The fact that we, like our Saviour, are called to serve rather than be served, rarely enters some people's heads.

Had Nehemiah's lieutenants opted for comfort, for easy living, for "nice services" and splendid programs they would have stayed in Susa, 'sunshine capital of Persia.' Instead, they saw an opportunity to serve and to use their spiritual gifts for God, and got on with the job.

Someone has well said that many of today's churches are made up of willing people: "those who are willing to work, and those who are willing to let 'em!" One preacher put it another way: "There are three types of Christians in most churches. First, are those who complain, 'Nothing ever happens around here'; second, those who inquire, 'Is anything happening around here?'; then there are those that 'make it happen!'" Paul would have appreciated that story. One of his aims in ministry was to encourage every member of the Body of Christ "To stir up the gift of God within them" and get functioning in fellowship with all the other members. Of course even in Nehemiah's group there were exceptions. We have bumped into them elsewhere – the "nobles" who *"would not put their shoulders to the work under their supervisors"* (3:5).

Here is the lesson for us today. Find a church where people are making things happen; where *"by love they serve one another"* (Gal. 5:13). Beware of the church that offers "something enjoyable for everyone." Find one that cries out, "Come and help us reach men and women for Christ." Then, join in, get involved and be prepared to put your shoulder to the wheel.

7. Celebration of Praise

There is an inspiring passage in the Book of Nehemiah which is all about singing. It has to do with the dedication of the completed wall. People had worked hard, stayed alert for the enemy and finished their God-given assignments. Now it was time for singing and praising.

We read,

> *"At the dedication of the wall of Jerusalem, the Levites were sought out from where they lived and were brought to Jerusalem to celebrate joyfully the dedication with songs of thanksgiving and with the music of cymbals, harps and lyres... I also assigned two large choirs to give thanks"* (Neh. 12:27, 31).

Evidently, the plan was for these two choirs to walk around the city walls, one group in one direction and one in the other. Then, as they met they assembled in the Temple for a celebration of praise. Everyone joined in, men, women and children. Indeed, so loud was the praise that, *"The sound of rejoicing in Jerusalem could be heard far away"* (12:43). Sounds like a church near where we used to live! It must have been a wonderfully joyous occasion as orchestra and choir sounded forth their paeans of praise to the Lord. By the way, is this incident saying to us again, Don't let your musical taste become a stumbling block to fellowship? Some like it loud, some don't, but all of us want to praise the Lord.

Music has always been an important element in biblical worship. People who have been redeemed and revived usually enjoy singing about it. Listen to Israel's famous song of praise — known in Jewish circles as "the *Hashirah*" — *"I will sing to the Lord, for He is highly exalted. The horse and its rider He has thrown into the sea. The Lord is my strength and my song; he has become my salvation. He is my God, and I will praise Him, my father's God and I will exalt him"* (Ex. 15:1-2 cf. also the ancient Song of Deborah in Judg. 5). Did Nehemiah perhaps have the words of Isaiah the prophet in mind as he enjoyed the 'praise project' that day?

> *"I will praise you, O Lord. Although you were angry with me, your anger has turned away and you have comforted me. Surely God is my salvation; I will trust and not be afraid. The Lord, the Lord, is my strength and my song; he has become my salvation. With joy you will draw water from the wells of salvation"* (Isa. 12:1-3).

It is unfortunate that our differences in musical taste tend to polarize us and inhibit our praise. True, crashing cymbals are not everyone's thing, but then neither are harps and lyres or even pipe organs! In Nehemiah's day, they all played and praised together and no one complained—unless it was some of their neighbours!

Without a doubt a renewed church will be a singing and a praising church. And, whether we appreciate the level of decibels or not, it is well to remember that God inhabits the praises of His people (Ps. 22:3). It is no accident that when Paul mentions some of the criteria of being *"filled with the Spirit"* he includes fellowship, continual thanksgiving and spontaneous praise. Of course, he also wisely suggests that two other factors should be kept in mind. One is that we "keep our minds in gear"—to paraphrase him. The other is to make sure our praise is directed to the Lord!

Here are the Apostle's inspired words,

> *"Do not get drunk on wine, which leads to debauchery. Instead, be filled with the Spirit. Speak to one another with psalms, hymns and spiritual songs. Sing and make music in you heart to the Lord, always giving thanks to God the Father for everything, in the name of our Lord Jesus Christ"* (Eph. 5:18-19).

> *"I will pray with my spirit, but I will also pray with my mind. I will sing with my spirit, but I will also sing with my mind"* (1 Cor. 14:15).

These then are a few of the hallmarks of genuine spiritual renewal that we discover in the Book of Nehemiah. We will not necessarily find all of them to the same degree in every local church situation. However, if none of them is found, or all are frowned on as undesirable, then almost certainly that place does not subscribe to the truth Nehemiah proclaimed, *"The joy of the Lord is your strength"* (Neh. 8:10).

PART III

STUDY SECTION

"They read from the Book of the Law, making it clear and giving the meaning so that the people could understand what was being read".
Nehemiah 8:8

CHAPTER FOURTEEN
THE CHRONOLOGY OF EZRA AND NEHEMIAH

The traditional view is that Ezra's return to Jerusalem preceded that of Nehemiah. The biblical text tells us that Ezra returned in the fifth month of the seventh year of King Artaxerxes (presumably Artaxerxes I, 464-424 B.C.)–that is 458/457 B.C. (see Ezra 7:8). Nehemiah came shortly after in the month Nisan, in the "twentieth year" of Artaxerxes I, that is 444 B.C. (Neh. 2:1ff). On this basis, Ezra arrived thirteen years before Nehemiah. However, since this chronology has been challenged on the basis of certain apparently discrepant details in the story, we will take a look at these contrary arguments. For a more detailed and careful discussion of this particular subject, the reader is recommended to consult Derek Kidner's commentary on Ezra — Nehemiah in the Tyndale Old Testament Commentary series (see the note at the conclusion of this chapter).

1. Ezra's delayed reading of the Law

Some argue that since Ezra is said to have arrived in Jerusalem in the seventh year of Artaxerxes to teach and implement the Law (Ezra 7:1,14; 8:10,25-26), and yet does not publicly read from the Law until the twentieth year of Artaxerxes, (Neh. 8:1ff) after Nehemiah's wall was complete, this suggests that the traditional order of Ezra first, Nehemiah second, should be reversed.

The argument goes on to suggest that the reference to the seventh year of Artaxerxes (Ezra 7:1) if correct, relates to Artaxerxes II. This would give a date of 398 B.C., obviously later than Nehemiah's arrival in 444 B.C. How are we to deal with this suggestion?

If this was Ezra's first public reference to the Law then the argument would be cogent. However, no such suggestion is made. In fact, the very reforms effected by Ezra were almost certainly accepted on the basis of his earlier instruction of the people out of the Law (see Ezra 9:10-11; 10:3 cf. 6:18). The whole story of reform in Israel witnesses to the fact that only when people were confronted with God's Word and Law did they change their ways.

The reason so much is made of the reading of the Law in Nehemiah chapter 8 is because of the significant, national occasion that is in view. It was the first civil New Year's celebration since the completion of the Jerusalem wall. The seventh month, Tishri, was not only the first month of the civil New Year, but the month of the Feast of Tabernacles, as well as the very important Day of Atonement, Lev. 23:26-36. Obviously, such a momentous occasion called for the special, six hour, religious ceremony and Law reading.

There is absolutely no evidence from the wording of Nehemiah chapter 8 either that this was Ezra's first public reference to the Torah or that this was a recently discovered legal document, as some more extreme critics suppose.

So we submit that this argument for reversing traditional chronology does not hold. For the same reason it is unnecessary, as it is sometimes proposed, to emend the text of Ezra 7:8 to read, *"Ezra arrived in Jerusalem in the fifth month of the twenty-seventh year of the king."*

2. The High Priest's family

Another argument put forward in support of the chronological priority of Nehemiah has to do with the family of Eliashib, the High Priest. The text indicates that Eliashib was a contemporary of Nehemiah's (Neh. 3:1; 10:23; 13:38). However, it is maintained on the basis of Ezra 10:6 as well as Nehemiah 12:11, that in Ezra's time, Jehohanan, Eliashib's grandson, was the high priest. If this evidence stands then obviously Ezra came later than Nehemiah.

Upon closer examination of the evidence we discover some interesting, related facts. First, the grandson of Eliashib in Nehemiah 12:11 is called Jonathan not Jehohanan and although these names sound similar their etymological roots are different. Second, Jehohanan was not the grandson of Eliashib as the foregoing argument claims. He was in fact his son, according to Nehemiah 12:23. Thirdly, Jehohanan is not called "high priest." This is only inferred from Ezra 10:6 which simply says, *"Ezra withdrew from before the house of God and went to the room of Jehohanan, son of Eliashib."*

What the text is saying is that, following his rather frenzied, public protest about the inter-marriage problem, Ezra retired to a nearby room which was usually occupied by the high priest's son. There, he continued his protest in the form of a private fast. That was a perfectly natural thing for a person such as Ezra to do. It says nothing about Jehohanan's status. As a son of the high priest and a priest himself, he would obviously live in the apartments allocated to the priestly clans. Again then, we see the argument is not valid.

3. The population of Jerusalem

Yet another proposed argument for Nehemiah's priority is that whereas in Nehemiah's time Jerusalem was sparsely populated (Neh. 7:4) by the time of Ezra it was crowded (Ezra 10:1).

Again, this is reading too much into the text. While it could be expected that a city's population might increase with the passing of time, this is certainly not inevitable, as anyone who has ever visited a Western "ghost town" will attest. Secondly, a more careful reading of Ezra 10:1 will show that the crowds in Jerusalem on the occasion in view consisted not of its regular citizenry but of people from all over the place who had been summoned to assemble under duress (Ezra 10:7-8). This argument really has no bearing on dating or sequence of events and would only be made by someone convinced of it on the basis of subjective criteria rather than objective data.

4. The problem of mixed marriages

This argument is based on the difference in the policies of Ezra and Nehemiah regarding the problem of mixed marriages. It supposes that since Ezra had faced the problem of mixed marriages and dealt with it summarily insisting on immediate divorces, it is unlikely that Nehemiah would have had to face the same situation a few years later. Further, it is stated that Nehemiah's gentler dealing with the miscreants he faced must have preceded Ezra's stronger reaction (see Ezra 10:9-15 and Neh. 9:1-2; 10:30; 13:23ff).

These are tenuous arguments to say the least, especially in light of normal human behaviour. Who is to say that however stringent the legislation may be, people will resist the urge to enjoy life's ordinary relationships? More than likely they would take advantage of whatever opportunities are available. Love is rarely subject to legislation and may even be challenged and encouraged by it. As far as the different responses of Ezra and Nehemiah are concerned, the explanation seems obvious— Ezra, as an important religious figure, was dealing with a national situation. Nehemiah's concerns were more localized. Without question, their basic intentions were the same even if their styles were markedly different. Each man was apparently effective, in his own way and time. Furthermore, while Ezra was seeking to rectify an already existing situation, Nehemiah was attempting to prevent a recurrence in a succeeding genera-tion. It is doubtful whether there is anything here that is signifi-cant chronologically, certainly nothing that suggests Nehemiah must have preceded Ezra.

5. Lack of association between Ezra and Nehemiah

Another argument which questions the traditional order of Ezra's and Nehemiah's respective ministries is based on their supposed lack of association with each other in what was apparently a common enterprise. It is argued that if Ezra and Nehemiah were both commanded by the same Persian mon-arch to become involved in the re-establishment of the retun-ing exiles in their own land, surely we should expect to find them working together. The answer to this is that while the scene of their ministry was the same, Jerusalem, their respect-ive commissions were different. Ezra's work was religious and social. As a priest, he was expected to effect the re-establish-ment of religious institutions and order. Nehemiah, on the other hand, was a civil servant, trained in political administration. He was appointed Tirshatha or governor and was sent to rebuild the city walls and establish civic order. There is no suggestion that Ezra and Nehemiah were strangers or in conflict with each other. Indeed, it is clear from Nehemiah 8:1ff. that, as governor, Nehemiah declined to overstep his bounds as a layman. He not only recognized Ezra's gifts and calling but encouraged him in his work. That they certainly worked together in enthusiastic cooperation is obvious from several passages. We read for example,

> *"Then Nehemiah the governor, Ezra the priest and scribe, and the Levites who were instructing the people said to them all, 'This day is sacred to the Lord your God. Do not mourn or weep.' For all the people had been weeping as they listened to the words of the Law. Nehemiah said, 'Go and enjoy choice food and sweet drinks, and send some to those who have nothing prepared. This day is sacred to the Lord. Do not grieve, for the joy of the Lord is your strength"* (Neh. 8:9-10).

We read further, *"They served in the days of Joiakim, son of Joshua, the son of Jozadak, and in the days of Nehemiah the governor and of Ezra the priest, and teacher of the Law"* (Neh. 12:26).

There is a particularly illuminating passage in the story of the dedication of the walls, which we looked at earlier. We read there that Nehemiah assigned "two large choirs to give thanks." Ezra was appointed to lead one choir and half of the congregation in one direction around the wall, while Nehemiah followed the other choir in the opposite direction. Eventually the massed choirs and the people came together at the Temple for a grand service of thanksgiving. Clearly Ezra and Nehemiah were in complete fellowship and accord (see Neh. 12:31-43).

6. The Elephantine Papyri (c. 5th Century B.C.)

The Elephantine papyri are a series of Aramaic documents dating from the fifth century B.C. They represent the correspondence of a Jewish military garrison that was established near the Southern border of Egypt. Apparently in one of the Elephantine papyri, usually dated 407 B.C., an appeal for help is made to "Delaiah and Shelemiah the sons of Sanballat governor of Samaria." A parallel reference suggests that these sons of Sanballat were contemporaries of Johanan, the high priest in Jerusalem. Those who argue for the Nehemiah—Ezra order relate this reference to Ezra 10:6 and see it supporting their contention that Ezra must have been in Jerusalem in 410 B.C., that is, thirty years after Nehemiah.

However, as noted above, Ezra 10:6 says nothing about Jehonan's holding the high priestly office in Ezra's time. The fact that he was mentioned as high priest in 410 B.C. simply confirms his existence. On the other hand the appeal to Sanballat's sons suggests that they were vice-regents and that their father was still living. This of course would mean that he was probably in his prime some twenty-five to thirty years earlier, and would make him a contemporary of Nehemiah's. That is precisely what we discover from Nehemiah chapters 4 and 5. Once again the evidence is ambivalent and fails to prove anything about the relative dates of Ezra and Nehemiah.

In summing up this discussion concerning the chronology of Ezra and Nehemiah, we cite two recognized, reliable authorities. The first, J. Stafford Wright, former Principal of Tyndale Hall, Bristol, writes,

> "There is therefore no necessity to rewrite history, and there is one strong, positive argument against the 398 redating of Ezra and Nehemiah, for there would have been many people living whose parents had seen Ezra and who would have told stories about him, but none whose parents had seen Nehemiah. The alternative date of 428 meets the Biblical requirement of having the two men as contemporaries.[1]"

The second, Derek Kidner, Warden of Tyndale House, Cambridge, writes,

---

[1]   J.S.Wright, "Book of Nehemiah," article in *Zondervan Pictorial Encyclopaedia of the Bible Vol. 4*, 407.

"In conclusion, it seems fair to say that none of the major or minor objections to the biblical order of events is compelling, and to point out that nothing stronger than probability is in fact claimed by most scholars for any of the suggested reconstruction. If that is the case, the narrative that we already have must surely take precedence over the narratives we do not have.[2]"

---

2   Derek Kidner, "Ezra and Nehemiah" published in *Old Testament Commentary* (Leicester, England: Inter-Varsity Press, 1979) 158.

APPENDIX ONE:
STUDY OUTLINES

The following study outlines are intended for use in Bible study groups and are based on the thirteen chapters of the Book of Nehemiah.

STUDY OUTLINE #1
FACING UP TO BAD NEWS

Reference: Nehemiah Chapter 1

Introduction

The events recorded in Nehemiah Chapter 1 took place about the middle of the 5th Century B.C., when the Persian empire was at its zenith. It is late fall, the month Kislev, equivalent to our November/December. Nehemiah, an outstanding leader in the community of Jewish exiles, is wintering in Susa, a city about 100 miles inland from the head of the Persian Gulf. He is the trusted leader of a minority group of exiles and is evidently part of the entourage of King Artaxerxes I.

One day Hanani, Nehemiah's brother, arrives from his distant homeland with the news that Jerusalem, the ancient centre of Judaism is little more than a derelict ruin. Nehemiah's instinctive reaction is to cast himself on God in prayer. More than half of this opening chapter is given over to his intercession. Here is a pattern for meaningful prayer.

Key Memory Verse: Nehemiah 1:4

> "When I heard these things, I sat down and wept. For some days I mourned and fasted and prayed before the God of heaven."

Study Questions:

1. How do you understand the term: "the Exile"?

2. What was the root cause of the Exile?

3. Can you name other famous members of the Exile?

4. Discuss the theology of Nehemiah's prayer.

5. What can we learn from Nehemiah's willingness to share the blame and confess to God?

6. Why does Nehemiah set such store by the Exodus and the giving of the Law?

7. What are important elements in Nehemiah's prayer?

STUDY OUTLINE #2
NIGHT TIME INSPECTION

Reference: Nehemiah Chapter 2

Introduction

In this chapter we see God's remarkable answer to Nehemiah's intercession. As Artaxerxes' cup bearer, Nehemiah had immediate, occasional access to the King. In fact, his position was both strategic and dangerous, as the story indicates.

Challenged by the king about his sad face, Nehemiah explains the plight of his homeland and boldly requests Artaxerxes' assistance. His request is generously heard and Nehemiah goes off with the king's authorization to rebuild the walls of Jerusalem and assist its distressed citizens.

Despite the rigours of the long and dangerous journey, upon his arrival in Jerusalem Nehemiah courageously sets about his formidable task and, despite opposition, succeeds. Wisely he undertakes his first inspection by night, aided no doubt, by the light of the Passover moon.

Key Memory Verse: Nehemiah 2:4

> *"The king said to me, "What is it you want?" Then I prayed to the God of heaven."*

Study Questions:

1. What do you think Nehemiah was doing in the four months between Kislev and Nisan? (see Neh. 1:1 and 2:1).

2. "When your knees knock kneel on them." How is that demonstrated in verses 1 to 4?

3. Explain the position, privileges and dangers of being a royal cupbearer.

4. What elements in Nehemiah's answer to the king indicate that he was a man of action as well as prayer?

5. To whom does Nehemiah attribute his success? What does that teach us?

6. What in this chapter indicates Nehemiah's qualification for leadership?

7. What does Nehemiah teach us about dealing with opposition?

STUDY OUTLINE #3
WORKERS TOGETHER

Reference: Nehemiah Chapter 3

Introduction

After making an assessment and taking careful inventory, Nehemiah encourages his fellow Jews to rebuild the walls and gates of Jerusalem.

This chapter is not just an uninteresting catalogue of names. It is an inspiring description of what happens when God's people get together and work. It is a reminder that while each one depends on the other, there is a definite allocation of responsibility. Priests, jewellers, perfume makers, men, women, rich, poor, famous and unknown - all pitched in to do God's work. Whether priests' palace, tower fortress or Dung Gate, every part was essential to the completeness and effectiveness of the whole. Notice how the city wall, gates and forts are mentioned in sequence, beginning with the Sheep Gate.

Key Memory Verse: Nehemiah 3:5

"The next section was repaired by the men of Tekoa, but their nobles would not put their shoulders to the work under their supervisors."

Study Questions:

1. What do you think inspired this unity in service?
2. What was the significance of "Gates" in an ancient city?
3. Can wall-building sometimes be considered "worship"?
4. What do you think about the *"nobles of Tekoa,"* (v. 5)?
5. What are tasks that can best be done by women?
6. How important is Christian unity?
7. Consider in context Paul's words *"workers together"* (see 1 Cor. 3:9).

STUDY OUTLINE #4
SWORDS AND TROWELS

Reference: Nehemiah Chapter 4

Introduction

In this chapter we see Nehemiah dealing with the insults and threats of his persistent enemies. On the one hand he wielded the weapon of "all prayer,"on the other he made sure his defences were secure round the clock and that his men were on guard.

Nehemiah evidently decided to build the entire wall to half its height. This was not only good strategy but wise psychology. It made everyone aware of the importance of their task and removed any suggestion of favouritism.

The idea of arming his workmen and employing them in shifts meant that enough people were alert and ready for action all the time.

Key Memory Verse: Nehemiah 4:20

"Wherever you hear the sound of the trumpet, join us there. Our God will fight for us!"

Study Questions:

1. Why were the Samaritans so opposed to the work?

2. Why is ridicule difficult to face?

3. How appropriate is it for Christians to pray as Nehemiah did (see, v. 4-5)?

4. In what ways should Christians be on guard?

5. Nehemiah set his men to work near their homes. Is there a lesson here about our families and homes?

6. Can we learn a lesson about Christian cooperation from v. 19-20?

7. What does Nehemiah's commitment have to teach us? (see v. 23).

STUDY OUTLINE #5
INTERNAL SQUABBLES

Reference: Nehemiah Chapter 5

Introduction

It was one thing to cope with the enemy, but in this chapter the problem is "division in the ranks." Apparently people who had money were taking advantage of their poorer compatriots. Greed and exploitation are nothing new but they are particularly reprehensible in families and in times of economic recession.

Nehemiah took strong measures to combat this unfortunate situation. First, he publicly condemned the miscreants and threatened to confiscate their property. Second, he put the community leaders under oath to "shape up or ship out." Added to this were his own generous gestures. On the one hand he lifted the burden of taxation and on the other he underwrote the expenses of his personal retinue.

Key Memory Verse: Nehemiah 5:16

> *"Instead, I devoted myself to the work on this wall. All my men were assembled there for the work; we did not acquire any land."*

Study Questions:

1. Why is greed so prevalent?
2. Is there anything wrong with taking out a mortgage?
3. Slavery is always evil. How did Mosaic legislation regulate it? see Leviticus 25.
4. How did Nehemiah's bring-it-into-the-open policy help?
5. When does profit taking become usurious?·
6. How important is a leader's example?
7. Hospitality is a forgotten art among many Christians. Why is this?

STUDY OUTLINE #6
INTIMIDATION TACTICS

Reference: Nehemiah Chapter 6

Introduction

It has often been pointed out that when God's work prospers, Satan is never far away. So in this story. Nehemiah's enemies, seeing his success and failing to abort his scheme, decide to harm him. On the surface their suggestions for a "Summit meeting" seem harmless enough but Nehemiah spots their trap.

The enemy tries all kinds of tactics such as flattery, intimidation, insinuation and innuendo, but Nehemiah stands his ground. He refuses to run. He will not desert his people nor his divine commission. It is worth noting that Nehemiah's enemies were not all militarists and politicians; some were religious pretenders. Little has changed.

Key Memory Verse: Nehemiah 6:3

> *"so I sent messengers to them with this reply: 'I am carrying on a great project and cannot go down. Why should the work stop while I leave it and go down to you?'"*

Study Questions:

1. "Finishing a job is much more important than starting one." How does this story illustrate that?

2. How can we be kept alert to Satan's schemes?

3. "I am carrying on a great project." What do Nehemiah's words tell us about the Lord's work?

4. What was the source of Nehemiah's strength?

5. How did his knowledge of scripture save the day for Nehemiah (v. 10-13)? What does this teach us?

6. How does success in the Lord's work affect our enemies?

7. How do we account for the unreliability of some of the Lord's people?

STUDY OUTLINE #7
KEEPING TAB

Reference: Nehemiah Chapter 7

Introduction

It is one thing to build the walls and gates of Jerusalem, it is another to make sure they are guarded. Nehemiah's plan was to reduce security breaches to a minimum by keeping the city gates closed until sufficient people were available to guard them.

Another sensible feature of Nehemiah's plan was to make people responsible for their own families and property. He also decided to take a census in order to make sure that everything was done "decently and in order." There are several genealogical tables and lists of names in this book (see Chapter 3 and 11:4-12:26). At first sight these may seem uninteresting and unimportant, but in Bible times such things were crucial. So much depended on the proper ordering of society.

Key Memory Verse: Nehemiah 7:2

> *"I put in charge of Jerusalem my brother Hanani, along with Hananiah the commander of the citadel, because he was a man of integrity and feared God more than most people do."*

Study Questions:

1. What were the two key features of Hanani's character that qualified him for responsibility?

2. Why is so little emphasis placed on integrity among Christians today?

3. What sort of things do we need to guard our homes and families against today?

4. Why are small churches often more "alive" than big ones?

5. Property, family and home were treated as a kind of divine stewardship in Israel. What can we learn from this?

6. Generosity in supporting God's work is commendable. Begging apart, how can we cultivate Christian giving?

7. Why is orderliness and good bookkeeping so helpful in the Lord's work?

STUDY OUTLINE #8
HEARING GOD'S WORD

Reference: Nehemiah 8

Introduction

This chapter is concerned with some important events which took place in the seventh month, one of particular significance in Israel's calendar. The seventh month, Tishri as it was called, was the beginning of the civil New Year, the setting of the Day of Atonement and the time for celebrating the Festival of Tabernacles.

This particular year, Nehemiah and Ezra decided to start right. They assembled the populace in the great public square near the Water Gate and held a six hour Bible reading! The effect was remarkable. There was praise, worship, mourning for sin and celebration. The Feast of Tabernacles was re-instated and there was almost unprecedented joy.

Key Memory Verse: Nehemiah 8:8

> *"They read from the Book of the Law of God, making it clear and giving the meaning so that the people understood what was being read."*

Study Questions:

1. Why is the Bible so important in any true revival?

2. Why are people so impatient and anxious to get church over these days?

3. There are several important things noted here regarding how the Word was read and presented. What are these? Can we learn from them?

4. Why do seminaries place so little stress on the careful, public reading of Scripture?

5. Two things characterized people who heard the Word of God - sorrow and joy. Explain this.

6. What was the Feast of Tabernacles all about?

7. Should we lay more emphasis on the celebration of the Lord's Supper?

STUDY OUTLINE #9
GREAT IS THY FAITHFULNESS

Reference: Nehemiah 9:1-37

Introduction

This chapter opens with another national gathering for the public reading of Scripture. On this occasion, two weeks after the last, the reading is accompanied by fasting, penitence and confession. The event took up half a day.

The major portion of verses 5-37, is devoted to a public prayer in which two themes intermingle. There is a celebration of God's acts throughout Israel's history and a confession of thieir disobedience and unfaithfulness. This historical resume begins with the election of Abram and comes down to their current situation. The prayer concludes with a pathetic recital of the exiles' predicament and the hope that God will not forget His covenant of love.

Key Memory Verse: Nehemiah 9:31

"But in your great mercy you did not put an end to them or abandon them, for you are a gracious and merciful God."

Study Questions:

1. Should fasting be given more prominence today?

2. Why is so little reference made to confession in most public prayers?

3. What divine attributes and characteristics are found in this great prayer?

4. Why do you think so much is said about the Egypt-to-Canaan phase of Israel's history but so little about the monarchy and captivity?

5. What parallels are there between God's dealings with Israel and with the Church today?

6. Is there enough acknowledgement of God's provision or are we tending to adopt an "I did it my way" attitude?

7. What do we believe about God's sovereignty in history?

STUDY OUTLINE #10
WE PROMISE...

Reference: Nehemiah 9:38-10:39

Introduction

Penitence is meaningless unless it has practical expression in our life. Here we see the Jerusalem community represented by their leaders, priests and Levites, subscribing their names to a covenant document. In it they pledge themselves to keep their part of the ancient Mosaic covenant. They bind themselves with curse as well as oath.

There are several particular items covered in this rededication document. They are: abstinence from mixed marriages and from trading on the Sabbath; recognition of sabbatical years; payment of poll tax and regular contributions for temple offerings as well as the ministry of priests and Levites.

Key Memory Verse: Nehemiah 10:35

"We also assume responsibility for bringing to the house of the Lord each year the firstfruits of our crops and of every fruit tree."

Study Questions:

1. Do you think it would be helpful to write down a reasonable statement of promise and commitment today?

2. Does the prohibition of mixed marriage have any continuing relevance?

3. While keeping the Sabbath is not binding today, are there principles and guidelines here for our behaviour on the Lord's Day?

4. "The Lord's people should support the Lord's work." Discuss this in the light of some of today's public begging.

5. Why is Christian giving so lamentable, generally speaking?

6. Is tithing all that is necessary today?

7. Our priority in giving should be the support of our own local Church (see v. 39). Do you agree?

STUDY OUTLINE #11
SINGING ON THE WALL

Reference: Nehemiah 11 and 12

Introduction

These two chapters are concerned with the establishment and maintenance of religious life in Jerusalem, which is here called, the Holy city. (11:18). One priority was to make sure there was a viable population. This was achieved by importing ten percent of the people from the rural areas. These were selected by casting lots and by soliciting volunteers. The entire section, 11:4-12:26, is taken up with the names and in some cases the tasks of the returned exiles who settled in Jerusalem and its environs. Some came from as far away as Beersheba (11:30). Over two thousand people are said to have been involved. Many no doubt were heads of families or clans. In any case, this list is not exhaustive, (cf. 1 Chron. 9). The second half of Chapter twelve is concerned with the dedication of the city walls and makes reference to two choirs and other Temple personnel. The two choirs evidently circled around the walls in opposite directions. The one was led by Ezra, the other was accompanied by Nehemiah. They met at the Inspection Gate (also known as the Guard Gate), then proceeded together to the temple for a Praise service.

Key Memory Verse: Nehemiah 12:40

> "The two choirs that gave thanks then took their places in the house of God; so did I, together with half the officials…"

Study Questions:

1. Consider the importance of commitment in God's service.
2. What makes Christians willing to forgo creature comforts?
3. Why do you think so many names are given?

4. What do you know about the Levites? How did they differ from priests?
5. How important is music in the Lord's work?
6. Why did leaders and people need "purifying"?
7. Why should full-time workers be supported by the Lord's people?

STUDY OUTLINE #12
CLEAN UP TIME!

Reference: Nehemiah 13

Introduction

While it is difficult to say exactly when these events took place, it was clearly following Nehemiah's twelve year absence from Jerusalem. Despite their earlier repentance and promises to serve the Lord in accordance with the Law, the people fell away.

Several things are symptomatic of Israel's apostasy. Tobiah the enemy was ensconced in the Temple precincts and that with the connivance of the High Priest! The Levites were no longer being supported and had to return to farming in order to make a living. The Sabbath was desecrated and mixed marriage with pagans was condoned.

Upon his return Nehemiah quickly rectified things. His methods were radical but effective and under God, he saved the day.

Key Memory Verse: Nehemiah 13:30

> *"So I purified the priests and the Levites of everything foreign, and assigned them duties, each to his own task."*

Study Questions:

1. Why was it important for God's people to separate themselves from unbelievers?
2. How can leaders of God's people become so spiritually obtuse?
3. What does Tobiah represent today?
4. When are Nehemiah's radical methods justified?
5. Are there times when we should speak out against the behaviour of non Christians?
6. How do you understand Nehemiah's seemingly self congratulatory prayers?

7. What warnings are in this chapter for Christians today?

APPENDIX TWO:
MAP OF NEAR EAST
AT THE TIME OF THE RETURN FROM EXILE

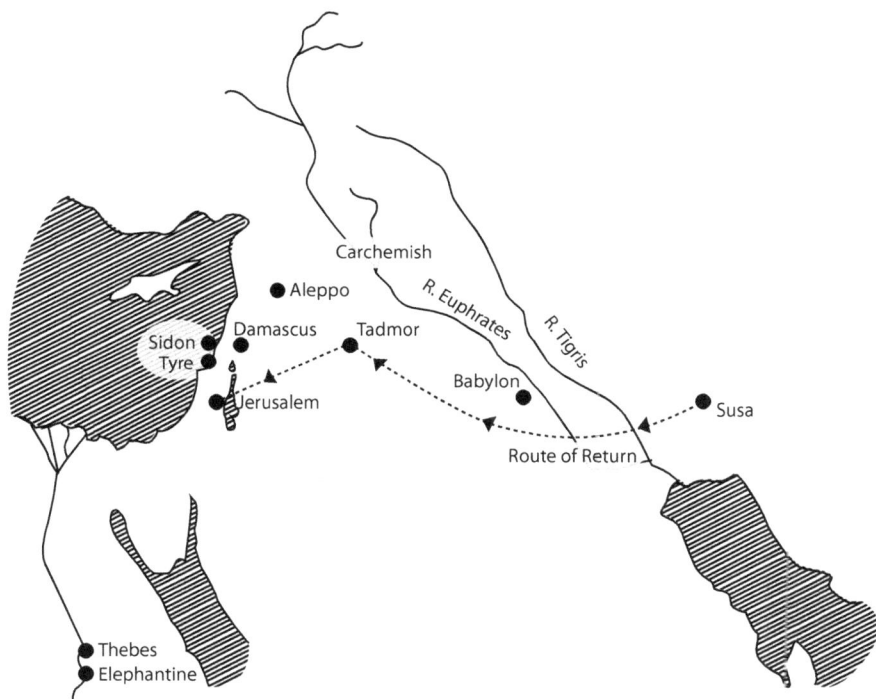

Carchemish

Aleppo

R. Euphrates

R. Tigris

Sidon
Tyre

Damascus

Tadmor

Babylon

Jerusalem

Susa

Route of Return

Thebes
Elephantine

APPENDIX THREE:
MAP OF JERUSALEM
& GATES IN NEHEMIAH'S DAY

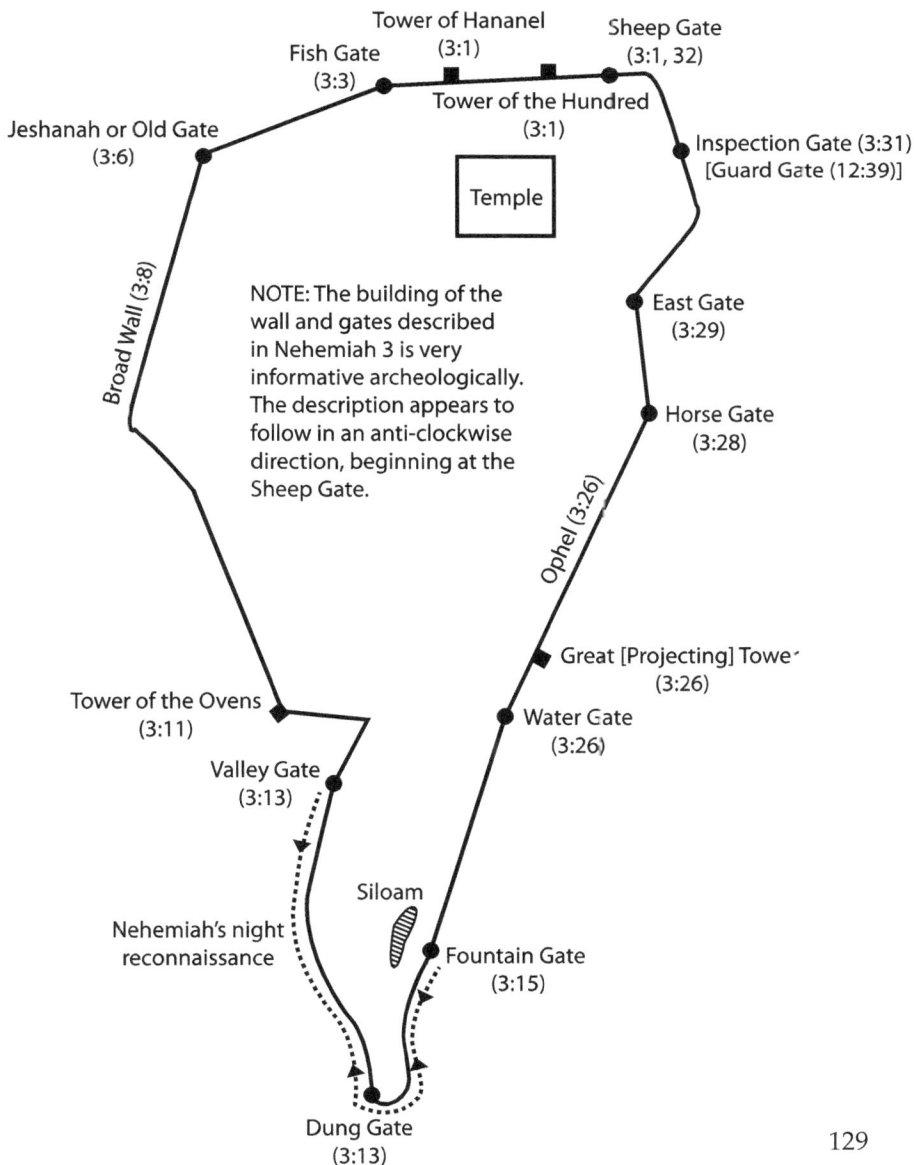

Tower of Hananel (3:1)

Sheep Gate (3:1, 32)

Fish Gate (3:3)

Tower of the Hundred (3:1)

Jeshanah or Old Gate (3:6)

Inspection Gate (3:31) [Guard Gate (12:39)]

Temple

Broad Wall (3:8)

East Gate (3:29)

Horse Gate (3:28)

NOTE: The building of the wall and gates described in Nehemiah 3 is very informative archeologically. The description appears to follow in an anti-clockwise direction, beginning at the Sheep Gate.

Ophel (3:26)

Great [Projecting] Tower (3:26)

Tower of the Ovens (3:11)

Water Gate (3:26)

Valley Gate (3:13)

Siloam

Nehemiah's night reconnaissance

Fountain Gate (3:15)

Dung Gate (3:13)

APPENDIX FOUR:
COMPARATIVE CALENDARS

Luni-Solar

Modern	Babylonia	Jewish	Jewish Feast	O.T. References
Mar.-April	Nisanu	Nisan-Abib	New Year (Relig.)	Ex. 12:2; Neh. 2:1;
			Passover (14th)	Ex. 12:14-20; Lev. 23:4
			Unleaven Br. (14-21st)	Ex. 12:17-20; Lev. 23:6
			Fristfruits (16th)	Lev. 23:9-14
April-May	Aiaru	Iyyar-Ziv	Pentecost or "Weeks" (6th)	Lev. 23:15-21
May-June	Simanu	Sivan		
June-July	Duzu	Tammuz		
July-Aug.	Abu	AB		
Aug.-Sept.	Ululu	Elul		
Sept.-Oct.	Tashritu	Tishri	New Year (Civil) 1st "Trumpets" Rosh Hashanah"	Lev. 23:23
			Day of Atonement (10th)	Lev. 16
Oct.-Nov.	Marcheshvan	Arahsamnu	"Tabernacles" 15-21st	

Modern	Babylonia	Jewish	Jewish Feast	O.T. References
Nov.-Dec.	Kislimu	Kislev	Hannukah "Lights" "Dedication"	(cf. John 10:22)
Dec.-Jan.	Tebetu	Tebeth		
Jan.-Feb.	Shabatu	Shebat		
Feb.-Mar.	Addaru	Adar	Purim	Est. 9:16

N.B.
An intercalary month — Adar-Sheni is added after three years (approx.)

CHRONOLOGICAL TABLE

Date (B.C.)	Event	Reference	Foreign King	O.T. Prophets	Era
722	Fall of N. kgdm. "Israel"	2 Kgs. 18:10	Shalmanezer V (726-722)	Isaiah Amos Hosea	Assyrian
612	Fall of Nineveh: Assyria				
597	Nebuchadnezzar v. Jerusalem			Habakkuk Jeremiah	
586	Fall of S. kgdm. "Judah" (Captivity in Babylon begins)	2 Kgs. 25:8	Nebuchad-nezzar (605-502)	Ezekiel Daniel	Babylonia
539	Fall of Babylon	Dan. 5:30	Cyrus (530-522)		
538	Cyrus' Decree to rebuild Jerusalem	Ezra 1:1			
536	Zerubbabel's ("Sheshbazzar") Return	Ezra 1:11 Ezra 2:2	Cambyses (530-522)		
536	Second Temple founded	Ezra 3:8-10		Haggai	
521	Darius' Decree		Darius I (521-486)	Zechariah	
521	Further Work on Temple	Ezra 5:2 Est. 1:1 Ezra 4:6	Xerxes I		
516	Temple Finished	Ezra 6:15	"Ahazuerus" (486-465)		Persian
458	Artaxerxes' Decree (1) to Ezra	Ezra 7:11	Artaxerxes I (464-424)		
458	Ezra's Return	Ezra 7:8			

BUILDING FOR GOD

Date (B.C.)	Event	Reference	Foreign King	O.T. Prophets	Era
445	Artaxerxes' Decree (2) to Nehemiah (20th year of Artaxerxes)	Neh. 2:99		Malachi	
444	Nehemiah's wall-building	Neh. 2:18ff			
432	End of Nehemiah's first term	Neh. 13:6	Darius II (423-404)		
432	32nd year of Artaxerxes	Neh. 5:14			
431	Nehemiah returns to Jerusalem		Artaxerxes II (404-359)		
332	Conquest of Persia by Alexander				Greek

MORE BOOKS:
BY JOHN WILLIAMS

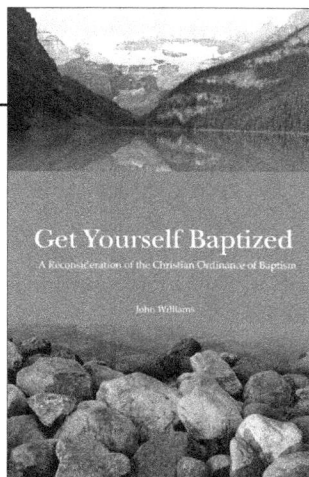

Get Yourself Baptized

A reconsideration of the Christian ordinance of baptism

Get Yourself Baptized offers a fresh look at an old topic. It underlines a Christian's responsibility to obey the Lord's Word and to have bold witness to his or her faith by getting baptized. Careful not to hurt feelings, the author is quite direct about what the Bible teaches on this important subject. The book will inform and challenge you to respond to Ananias' words, first spoken to the new convert, Saul of Tarsus; *"What are you waiting for? Get yourself baptized"* (Acts 22:16).

ISBN: 9781926765426
Pages: 124

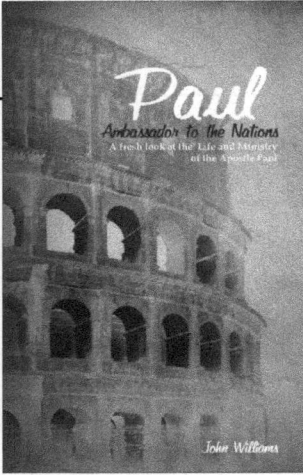

Paul: Ambassador to the Nations

A fresh look at the Life and Ministry of the Apostle Paul

"Another book about the Apostle Paul?"—you may ask. Yes, but one written from a different perspective. This is not a biography, nor is it an outline of Pauline theology. In these chapters we shall see Paul "wearing his many different hats," and functioning in a wide variety of settings. Hopefully, we shall identify with the Apostle, at least to some degree, then seek to follow his noble example. Do you aspire to be a preacher, a teacher, pastor, elder, deacon, Sunday School helper or youth worker? Do you sense God calling you to missionary service? Are you gifted as a church planter or a pioneer in some corner of the harvest field? Has God gifted you as a writer or a thinker, someone able to help us understand the great concepts of Scripture and Christian theology? Or, perhaps you see yourself as, "just one of those ordinary members of the Body of Christ," who help make things tick.

However you choose to answer those questions, please be assured that Paul, the bond-slave of Jesus, has something important to say to you.

ISBN: 9-780830-746897
Pages: 164

Festival of Remembrance and Hope

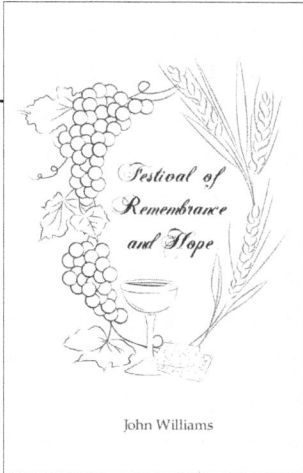

A study focused on the Breaking of Bread: The Lord's Supper

Festival of
Remembrance
and Hope

John Williams

What a special privilege it would be, to be invited to dine with her Majesty Queen Elizabeth II. This book will tell us that, as Christians, ours is a much greater honor. We are invited to eat and drink in the Presence of the King of Kings! For the Lord's Supper is not just a religious ceremony but an opportunity to fellowship with the Lord Jesus and his people. As you read through these pages you will discover the deep meaning and blessing resulting from accepting Jesus' invitation, "Do this for a remembrance of me." His special meal, though simple in its elements is sacred in its celebration. *Festival of Remembrance and Hope* will move your mind to wonder and your heart to worship as you reflect on the magnificent grace of God, revealed in the saving death and glorious resurrection of our Living Lord. "Here , O our Lord, we see Thee face to face; Here would we touch and handle things useen;" (Horatius Bonar).

ISBN: 9-781926-765259
Pages: 160

Visions of Messiah

A devotional study on the prophecies in the book of Isaiah

Visions of Messiah is a devotional exposition of the wonderful drama of God's saving grace and glory as it is unfolded in the magnificent Prophecy of Isaiah. Written for the ordinary reader, as well as those who are called to expound the treasures of God's Word to His people, this book will inform your mind and touch your heart. It is the Apostle John who tells us that Isaiah saw a vision of Christ in glory and was inspired to "go and tell" (John 12: 37-41). Let these pages move you to worship; then say, "Lord, here am I. Send me!"

ISBN: 9-781897-117743
Pages: 134

www.ingramcontent.com/pod-product-compliance
Lightning Source LLC
Chambersburg PA
CBHW060017050426
42448CB00012B/2794